FAITH AFTER FORTY

FAITH AFTER FORTY

Simple Steps to Stronger Faith

BRION SCOTT JOHNSON

Shoreline Arts & Publishing, LLC

Hinsdale, Illinois

Shoreline Arts & Publishing, Hinsdale 60521

Shoreline Arts & Publishing, LLC., Illinois

Copyright © 2009 by Brion Scott Johnson

All rights reserved. Published 2009

Cover photo © 2009 by Brion Scott Johnson

www.brionscottjohnson.com

Printed in the United States of America

IBSN: 978-0-615-32626-9

For Sandy, Courtney and Riley

Contents

INTRODUCTION

I am writing this introduction in March, 2009, during the worst financial crisis since the Great Depression and the worst economic slump in decades. Like many people, I am unemployed, although this reflects a conscious decision to quit my job about eight months ago, rather than any misfortune. My primary focus since resigning my position has been writing this book. I also have spent some time developing my skills in drawing and painting. This is a blessing, because I was in the investment management business and the world of investment management has been in turmoil virtually ever since I left my position. In contrast, I have been able to enjoy the fruitful contemplation of writing and some growth in my art, a lifelong interest that I had little time to pursue in the previous twenty years.

As you can tell from the title, this book is about faith, and it is particularly directed at people who are in what has commonly been called the "second half" of their lives. Of course, I am one of those people. Maybe you have enjoyed some material success, but you feel that something is missing from your life. Or perhaps you are surprised that you have grown in so many ways, but your faith life has not kept pace with the rest of your development. My hope is that you will realize that the same energy and enthusiasm that have helped you mature in other areas of your life can be brought to your faith life and used to deepen your relationship with God. In a sense, this book is a celebration of the fantastic opportunity that middle age represents: the chance to take stock of one's life—and if necessary, to make changes—with the hope that those changes bring us nearer to our utmost creative potential, which is to say nearer to God.

I undertook this examination of my life more fully as I was approaching my fortieth birthday. What I discovered was that I was reasonably happy with just about every aspect of my life, except for my spiritual life. Sure, I went to church every weekend, but I did not feel like my faith was a central part of my life. Going to church had become routine, my prayer life was not much more than rote recitation and, to be perfectly honest, my entire concept of God had become vague and noncommittal. Sadly, I was not really troubled by this, because my life was otherwise going very well. It took some real introspection before I recognized that, although I was happy, I was not satisfied. Something important seemed to be missing from my life, despite my obvious blessings.

Reflecting on all of this, I made a conscious decision to come to terms with my faith, and I embarked on a nearly ten-year journey that has proved transformational. All of the things mentioned above have changed: weekly worship is exhilarating; my prayers have become more like daily conversations with God; and my relationship with God has become more personal. This book is about that journey and the spiritual disciplines I found most helpful in opening myself up to God, so that He could cause all of these changes—and a whole lot more.

INTRODUCTION

I believe that faith is a gift from God. In that sense, there is nothing we can do to gain faith. However, I also believe there are some things that we can do to increase our receptivity to God's gifts, including the gift of faith. When we do that, our faith deepens. The things that worked best for me are the subject of the later chapters of this book.

Importantly, while there are actions we can take to facilitate our relationship with God, our sights should always be on God and not on the things we do, lest they become rituals that interfere with the more intimate relationship God offers us. That relationship is accessed by acknowledging the need for God in our lives and repenting for the sins that separate us from God. Once we take those steps, we are transformed into a new creation, as if we have been born again.

But what if we do that and nothing seems to happen? What if nothing seems to change? What if we have always believed, but we have relegated our faith to a subordinate role in our lives, as I had, to little more than going to church on Sundays? Eventually, we'll notice that something is missing. No matter how successful we are, or how much money we have, the world just won't seem like enough. We might feel a little empty, or more likely, we'll quicken the pace of our lives in order to fill up that emptiness, without even recognizing it is there. While this might work for a time, and it may produce material success as a consequence, nothing can take the place of God in our lives. So, until we open ourselves up to God, our striving will tend to increase and our unsatisfied longings will only deepen.

FAITH AFTER FORTY

As the current environment helps to illustrate, material things are poor substitutes for God. For many people, the current financial crisis has eviscerated years of hard work. Many may be starting all over again, with nothing except the wisdom of the experience. Things hoped for may have vanished in what seems like the blink of an eye. The road ahead may seem long, and many, no doubt, feel weary. But, as we read in the Bible, God offers us rest.

When we are able to rest in God, environments like the one we are in right now seem temporary and far less cause for concern. We begin to see them as an invitation for deeper faith, or perhaps as a reminder of the consequences of the lack of faith, or both. Regardless, it becomes an opportunity to exercise faith, and in so doing, come closer to God.

That is not to say that faith leads to complacency. I find myself reading the newspapers for signs of economic turnaround and for signals as to how I should invest just as intently as I did before, but without the collateral concerns that previously accompanied such activities. I am confident that whatever ultimately happens, it is God's will, or that God's will can be brought to those circumstances, and that is enough for me. I hope that you, too, find the faith and security only God can offer.

Brion Scott Johnson

Hinsdale, Illinois

CHAPTER ONE

WHAT IS FAITH?

JESUS REPLIED, "I TELL YOU THE TRUTH, IF YOU HAVE FAITH AND DO NOT DOUBT, NOT ONLY CAN YOU DO WHAT WAS DONE TO THE FIG TREE, BUT ALSO YOU CAN SAY TO THIS MOUNTAIN, 'GO, THROW YOURSELF INTO THE SEA,' AND IT WILL BE DONE. IF YOU BELIEVE, YOU WILL RECEIVE WHATEVER YOU ASK FOR IN PRAYER." (MATTHEW 21:21-22)

What would you be willing to do for God? Assuming anything was possible, what would you be prepared to achieve for God? In Mark 9:23 we read, "Everything is possible for him who believes," so this notion of incredible possibilities for the faithful has grounding in the Bible. Yes, faith can help us in our weakness, but it offers much more.

The Bible also tells us that "without faith, it is impossible to please God" (Hebrews 11:16). Speaking personally, I am at my best when I am quietly centered in my faith; in contrast, I do not always like the person I become when my faith is flagging. In the first instance, I am imaginative, accepting, and confident. In the latter, I am more linear, circumspect, and striving.

Not only is faith at the center of our relationship with God, it also affects our relationships with others—and, as the previous paragraph attempted to convey, even with ourselves. If we are going to get these important relationships right, then we need to make faith a priority. This book is about how an ordinary person—as opposed to one unusually spiritually-gifted—deepened his Christian faith. By sharing my story, I hope to provide some reassurance that God will respond if you are earnest in seeking Him.

Returning to the question that is the title of this chapter, the Merriam-Webster Dictionary offers the following definitions of faith: "**1 a:** allegiance to duty or a person : loyalty **b** (1): fidelity to one's promises (2): sincerity of intentions **2 a** (1): belief and trust in and loyalty to God (2): belief in the traditional doctrines of a religion **b** (1): firm belief in something for which there is no proof (2): complete trust **3:** something that is believed especially with strong conviction; ESPECIALLY : a system of religious beliefs <the Protestant FAITH>." Inherit to faith then is strong conviction, belief, complete trust, and loyalty; and inherent to loyalty is the idea of being willing to follow and to obey.

"When I grow up, I want to be a follower." Do you remember saying that when you were younger? Me neither. At one level, we all want to be "self-made" and self-determined. We admire hard work and persistence. We want to be self-reliant and to forge our own destinies. We don't want to follow; we want to lead, so we dismiss the basic message of the Bible.

Being agents of change, we may mold our faith into something that serves us better than this notion of "following." We use phrases like "God helps those who help themselves" to reinforce our belief that our self-determinism is part of our spiritual DNA. However, that phrase is not actually found in the Bible. Rather, the very consistent message of the Bible is that we have to be willing to FOLLOW God and to place our reliance TOTALLY on Him.

Personally, I struggled with this. Sometimes I still do. I struggled because I defined myself too narrowly as someone trying to move from the lower rungs of the economic ladder to the higher rungs. I struggled because I was somewhat successful at this, so I was not always mindful about what I was missing along the way. I struggled because I was connected almost wholly to the mental, physical and socio-economic dimensions of my existence; as a result, I had lost touch with the spiritual dimension of my life. And I struggled because the consistent message I received from the world was that I was "successful" in what I was doing; therefore, everything was just fine.

Despite all of these affirming indications, deep down, I knew that something was missing. Recognizing this about a decade ago, I began a much more intentional journey of faith. This book is about that journey and the spiritual disciplines I found personally effective. This book is also the next step on that journey, which is to share with you God's blessing of faith. But this book is much more than that. It is my expression of gratitude to God for the opportunity to become faithful without the trials and tribulations that sometimes seem to precede deepening faith. God reaches out to us always, and we can choose to reach back at any time in our lives, good or bad. When we do, God responds.

In a sense, faith asks a question: What would you be willing to do for God? Will you follow where He leads, even if the road looks difficult? Would you leave your job in the middle of a housing crisis, in a very uncertain economy, just as the market entered bear market territory, and the economy was poised for recession and the worst financial crisis since the Great Depression?

What if you believed God wanted you to do so? Would you leave behind hundreds of thousands of dollars in all but certain earnings and benefits, even more to the upside, if you believed it was God's will for you?

That is exactly what I did. I set aside my career and began to write this book, even though I was not an author and I had never written a book. I left my job having only a vague idea of what I might say—and absolutely no idea whether the book might be published. I left believing that it would, in all likelihood, adversely affect my career. I left even though my career was one that I had managed carefully and somewhat successfully up to that point in time; in fact, advancing my career had been one of the more important aspects of the prior twenty years of my life. Most importantly, I left without having a precise idea of the effect it would have on my family. What rational person, responsible for two children and a wife, would do such a thing?

As I write this, it is July 10, 2008, about a week after my last day in the office and about a month since I resigned my position as executive vice president in charge of public fixed income and portfolio management for a successful, Chicago-based asset management company that managed over seventy-eight billion dollars in assets. Yes, that is *billion*, including what is reported to be the largest retail high yield ("junk bond") mutual fund in Japan.

When I left, I received a terrific send-off from my colleagues who, although they didn't really understand what was motivating me, wished me well. Whenever I answered the question "So what are you going to do?" my answer was necessarily vague: "I'm going to take the summer off and spend some time at the summer house on Lake Michigan with the kids. I have this book rattling around my head I think that I have to write. After that, I'm not exactly certain." People always wanted to know more about the book, but at the time I didn't have much to add.

As will become very clear, I am not a Bible scholar. There are many people far better qualified to write about faith. However, I know enough to be certain that when we sincerely believe God has called us to do something, we have to have the faith to listen and the will to obey; and I am reasonably certain God wants me to write this book. So, here I am, writing. When we sincerely believe God asks something of us, and we have taken the steps to ascertain that it is truly His will, we have to obey; that is the essence of faith. It just doesn't go well for us when we take any other path.

Remember what happened when Adam and Eve didn't listen to the ONE THING God asked them NOT to do? They could eat of the fruit of any other tree in the garden, but the one forbidden tree became the sole focus of their attention.

But, there is no reason to single them out. When I type the phrase "disobedience to God" into my Bible software, five thousand references come up. *5000!* Thankfully, we stopped writing these things down centuries ago. Think about the events and circumstances we can point to today that show the

9

consequences of not listening to God. Five thousand infractions is a drop in the ocean, isn't it?

We human beings are quite practiced in not listening to God. But the consistent message of the Bible is that God keeps acting in our lives. He won't let us go off on our own and forget about Him. He wants a relationship with us, so He just keeps prodding us until we begin to listen. In time, we may even choose to do what He says. In my case, it took me over eight years to respond to this particular call.

I first had the idea for this book (or, perhaps, the idea for this book was first given to me) about eight years ago, while reading the Bible. The title seemed to just drop into my head, and my subsequent reading and the spiritual practices of my life seemed to follow. However, I had better things to do than write a book about my journey toward God. Most of those "things" centered in "succeeding" in this world as so many of us often define success, which is to say primarily monetarily. I now believe that God wouldn't let it stop at that. He wanted me to begin writing. And what I found out was that the cost of not listening to God was going up every year. My career was going well and my income was rising commensurately, so that at every point in time the cost of taking the time out to write the book was getting higher for me, because God was richly blessing me along the way. I finally realized that it was my turn to respond, so I resigned my position and resolved to write.

When my resignation was announced, my colleagues were stunned. One of them asked me, "Did you think about this before you did it?" Another asked, "Why would you leave now, when you've got things running so well?" One, a Christian, intimated that it was possible that the call I was hearing was the work of the devil. This was a bit unnerving, but I was reassured the very next day in a conversation with a devout Jewish colleague. He noted that the devil tempts us with things that are easy to do. Leaving behind much of what I worked for certainly was not easy. He related the oral tradition of his faith surrounding the call to Abraham to sacrifice Isaac, and the many difficulties that Abraham encountered while trying to obey. A couple of days after this conversation, Abraham was the topic of the sermon given at the church we attended in Michigan. That "coincidence" was one of many that assured me that the conversation with my colleague was God-given.[1] In fact, I received many signs in the days following my decision to resign that affirmed my belief that this calling was genuine.

Do you have the kind of faith to leave behind the familiar and to go where God calls you? Do you even want it? I didn't want it the day after I quit my job! Then God started sending me affirming messages, like those I mentioned above. Because of the nature of my work, they came, quite literally, from all over the world. Soon, I realized that I and my family would be okay despite my decision to leave my career behind for awhile. Perhaps we would even be better for it, as least as far as God is concerned.

It is amazing how God will speak to you if you listen. It is a little scary, too, to be honest, but it is amazing indeed.

But, I am way ahead of myself. You can tell that I am not a typical author, because I started this book at the end. This is not about my decision to follow what I believe was God's call to write; it is about certain spiritual disciplines that help us to develop the ability to listen and the faith to obey when God tells us to do something—even if our brains, our relatives, our friends, and our some of our colleagues intimate that what we're doing makes no sense at all. My hope is that this story—the story of a typical person seeking God—and the things I discovered along the way, may help you in your faith journey.

DISCUSSION/STUDY QUESTIONS FOR CHAPTER ONE

1. The dictionary definition of faith invokes words like "loyalty," "sincerity," and "trust." Inherent to the definition is being willing to follow where God leads. What is God calling you to do that you might be resisting?

2. In what ways is our "can do" culture a hindrance to the notion of following? How might it encourage you to take responsibility for cultivating your faith?

3. Our lives have various dimensions – mental, physical, social and spiritual. What practices can you adopt to ensure some consistency in the development of your spiritual life?

4. Generally, we are awkward beginners before we become really good at something. How much time do you give your faith life? What disciplines do you employ to grow in your faith? Does anything in particular hinder your desire or ability to grow spiritually?

5. Is a relationship with God "missing" from your life? Does the entire concept of such a relationship seem alien or strange to you? Why do some people seem so secure in their faith and so certain that such a relationship exists?

6. Can material success be an obstacle to faith? How can it cause faith to grow?

CHAPTER TWO

MY SPIRITUAL BEGINNINGS

YOUR EYE IS THE LAMP OF YOUR BODY. WHEN YOUR EYES ARE GOOD, YOUR WHOLE BODY ALSO IS FULL OF LIGHT. BUT WHEN THEY ARE BAD, YOUR BODY ALSO IS FULL OF DARKNESS. SEE TO IT, THEN, THAT THE LIGHT WITHIN YOU IS NOT DARKNESS. THEREFORE, IF YOUR WHOLE BODY IS FULL OF LIGHT, AND NO PART OF IT IS DARK, IT WILL BE COMPLETELY LIGHTED, AS WHEN THE LIGHT OF A LAMP SHINES ON YOU.
(LUKE 11:34-36)

To provide some context for reading, I would like to tell you a little bit about myself. What should become clear is that there is nothing particularly special, "spiritual," or even all that interesting about me. The fact is that my upbringing is that of an everyman: a typical middle-class American with typical middle-class values and no unusual ecumenical training. As the Bible articulates in story after story, God can work with whatever we present to Him.

The reality also presented in the Bible is that even the most faithful, with the notable exception of Jesus, are never quite ready to do God's bidding. The Bible is full of stories of people refusing God's call. Even Moses, a historical figure revered by Jews, Christians, and Muslims alike, did not feel ready to serve when he was called.[2] The message of the Bible is clear: God's love for us is greater than we can imagine, and He will provide for us if we step out in faith. Another thing that becomes painfully clear—brought most sharply into focus at Calvary—is that God's bidding may not be easy.

As you learn more about me, you may be impressed with the notion that I am not exactly a big risk-taker. Indeed, in many ways, my life has been very programmatic, logically leading from one thing to the next, with reasonably consistent progress along the way. The chances that I have taken, with the exception of this one, typically have been quite calculated. Given my naturally cautious nature, I can only conclude that it is God who provided the will for me to take the risk to drop everything and to write.

Finally, what I hope will become clear is that I am a pretty rational person; I didn't suddenly lose my mind and start hearing voices in my head telling me to do this. Despite some arguments to the contrary, rational, thinking people can choose to follow God. But we need to invest the time to "be still" in order to hear His call. When we hear that call and step out in faith, God's blessings really begin to flow.

Writing this book and the entire process around it, most especially how my wife, Sandy, has supported me in the endeavor, have been a blessing that I never could have imagined. God's good work in my life continues because I heeded His call, just not in ways that I had expected. My life is much better for having taken this leap of faith, and my hope for you is that you will experience the same.

By way of background, I grew up on the near-south side of Chicago, in "Mayor Daley's neighborhood," commonly called "Bridgeport." When I wrote "Mayor Daley," it was in reference to the father of the current mayor of Chicago, who lived there while he served as mayor, but I could just have easily been referring to the man who holds the office today, because he grew up there, too. We lived almost exactly five blocks north of the mayor on the same street, Lowe Avenue. There were six children in my family, five boys and a girl. People always ask, so I will tell you: my sister was the second child. In birth order, we went: Boy, girl, boy, boy, boy, boy.

Oh boy! Sometimes, I can't imagine how my parents managed their way through so many children. I was the fourth child, which is the middle boy.

For most of my youth, we rented a two-bedroom apartment that took up half of the top floor of a typical Chicago, brick, two-story building. My parents, God bless them, slept on a pull-out couch, and somehow found a way for the two small bedrooms to accommodate all six of us children. We moved down to the first floor, and a lot more space, when the landlord's children were grown and had left the house.

The area where we lived was composed predominately of Italian families, although there were a lot of Irish there as well, in part because of our extended family. My maternal grandmother lived three houses south of where we lived. Above her lived my mother's next older sister, her husband and their family of five children. On the other half of the top floor of the building in which we lived was my mother's oldest sister, her husband and their five children. We never had a small party when I was growing up, because just inviting the immediate family guaranteed a pretty large group of people.

In terms of religious affiliations, my mother is Catholic and my father is agnostic. This is today as it was when we were growing up, although some recent conversations with one of my siblings suggest that perhaps my father's agnosticism has devolved into atheism. I suppose, as one of my Christian former coworkers suggested, my dad's lack of faith is one of the reasons I am writing this book. Maybe after reading this and we have talked some more, he'll give it another thought. I would be overjoyed if he did.

Thankfully, my parents are both alive. Now in their eighties, they live in the house that used to be owned by my grandmother, right there in Bridgeport, three houses away from where we lived when I was growing up.

My father grew up in Pasadena, California and my mother grew up in Chicago—in Bridgeport—where she has lived her entire life. In this way, I suppose I am more like my mother than my father, never having lived farther away from home than Michigan. Still, that makes me a bit of an adventurer in my family, as I am the only one in my immediate family who has ever lived outside of the Chicago-area.

We attended Catholic schools, even though they were more expensive than public schools, because my mother wanted us raised Catholic and my father was not impressed by the Chicago school system, which really wasn't that good at the time. Accordingly, I have been Christian as long as I can remember, although my faith, until much later in life, was more or less something that I "did" on Sundays.

This did not reflect a failing of the Catholic Church or my parents, but what I had thought of as a predisposition for pragmatism that I had at a very early age. With the benefit of more time, I have concluded that it also may have reflected a lack of awareness of the importance of spiritual matters that did not change much until about ten years ago, when I began earnestly reading my Bible.

In terms of economic status, I suppose that we would have been considered "middle class" or perhaps lower middle class, because we did not own the house in which we lived. At the risk of sounding cliché, I can say that our family was rich in the things that really mattered. This is true primarily because my mother did not work outside of our home. So, we were living on one income, but we were raised full-time by a truly remarkable woman.

My father modeled a work ethic that in some ways molded my own; he shunned the patronage jobs available to those residing in that area of the city for work that he obtained on his own terms. Even though it was harder and less lucrative than the afore-mentioned patronage jobs, he had the satisfaction of knowing that he was contributing more meaningfully to GDP. (I cannot wait for the uproar that the last sentence might kick up! Yes, I know that the government provides necessary services, but there was no question that patronage in Chicago at the time, and perhaps now, if the press is to be believed, provided a lot of people with the opportunity to produce little and obtain a lot of money and benefits in return.)

My mother was a five-foot-two-inch dynamo. She never stopped moving. Despite having six children, five of them boys, our house was always spotless. She still is a dynamo, but a bit less than five-feet-two now because of her age. A simple story illustrates the sort of person that she is. One day when I was about twelve and we were living in the larger quarters mentioned earlier, she decided to paint the family room. It was a large room. My guess is that it was about 15'x15'. The ceilings in that house were probably about eleven-feet high. She painted the entire room, all by herself, while we were at school. The next day, after deciding that she did not like the new color of the room, she repainted it! When she wanted something done, she waited for no one; she just did it, and long before Nike® coined the phrase.

My father is in many ways a uniquely blessed individual. When we were younger, I can remember my father saying more than once that he "could do anything." As far as I can tell, that was true. As a young man, he earned a scholarship to university, although he did not go because his parents divorced and my dad went to work to help support his family. He was good enough as an artist to draw for Disney part-time when he was a young man. About a day before he was too old to be drafted into military service, he was drafted into the army, during the Korean conflict. Although he was obviously among the oldest of the recruits, he was the number one marksman among a unit of eleven thousand men, and he ended up teaching hand-to-hand combat and weapons to other soldiers.

He could fix anything that was broken, and he was the only person who could keep our twelve-year-old station wagon moving when we were children. At some point, no one else would even work on it. He quotes Shakespeare, and he has knowledge of classical music that goes back to his high school days in Pasadena, which, evidently, had phenomenal schools at that time. He has an extraordinary combination of natural skills, both physical and intellectual and, at eighty-three years old, he is still the person to have on your team if you want to have a shot at winning the family ping-pong or billiards competition.

We lived half a city block from the first grammar school I attended, which was on the second floor of the Catholic church we attended at the time. Reflecting its poor monetary condition, the school was closed after I completed second grade. I was drafted as an altar boy in that year, because the church remained open but, owing to the school's closing, it had lost the pool from which altar boys were drawn. I served at that church through my freshman year in high school, not because of any strong spiritual calling, but primarily because they needed me and it seemed like the right thing to do.

After the school closed, we switched to another Catholic school a little farther away that I attended through fifth grade. We switched again because of the expense to another Catholic school a little more than a mile from home, where I graduated from elementary school. Each of these schools was alongside of a church, and religious studies and attendance at church were part and parcel of my Catholic education.

You can guess from the above description that Bridgeport was full of churches. Curiously, at one time, the neighborhood's reputation was that it had more churches and bars per square mile than any other place in Chicago. I don't know whether this was true or urban legend, but it certainly seems possible based on my recollection.

Upon graduation from elementary school, we moved to yet another Catholic school, St. Ignatius College Prep, which was run by the Jesuits. Having attended some pretty solid educational institutions since then, I am convinced that they may be among the best educators in the world. However, I have also come to appreciate more fully our parents' role in teaching us some of the more important lessons of life.

As you might expect, a private, college preparatory education does not come cheaply. My brothers and I caddied during the summers to help pay for our tuition. A few of us also slung mops over the school floors during the academic year, until we were old enough and better qualified for labor that paid better. It was what our parents expected us to do and, personally, I don't feel any worse off for having done it. As a nation, we seem to want to level the playing field for every bit of difference in socio-economic status that inevitably confronts us, but I am convinced that the work ethic my parents encouraged produces a better long-term result. It is the difference between giving a man a fish and teaching him to fish, and I am grateful for the teaching.

Sometime in my freshman or sophomore year of high school, a Jesuit priest took an interest in my spiritual development. I am not sure why he chose me for the program, whether he noticed some receptivity or whether he saw dire need. I suspect that it was for the former reason, but it is of little consequence. We met a couple of times a week for the next few weeks after school. I don't recall exactly how it happened, but I think that it is safe to say that at some point he got frustrated with trying to lead me spiritually. He let me know that I needed to express more, or perhaps a different, interest in what we were doing, or I would have to move on. I thought that his change of heart was rather abrupt, and that his attitude was less than friendly about the whole matter, so I chose to move on. As a result of this decision and my not seeking a substitute for his spiritual guidance, throughout high school my spiritual undertakings remained limited to attending church on Sundays. In school, I took classes in world religions and philosophy, but those were motivated more by intellectual interest than anything else.

I don't remember ever praying, except at mass or perhaps when I had to give a speech in class. I hated public speaking at the time. As if it were the only reason to pray, I don't remember ever thinking that I needed God's help anyway. Getting good grades was pretty easy for me, and that seemed to be the primary focus of just about everyone around me.

Things did not change much in my early adult life. For my undergraduate education, I attended the University of Michigan as an Evans Scholar. One aspect of the scholarship is that students live with other Evans Scholars in a house very similar to a fraternity. The primary difference is that you don't get to choose your housemates; you live with other people awarded the scholarship. Not at all by chance, but by the hand of Providence, I met some terrific Christian men there. In fact, one of them was assigned to be my "big brother" by virtue of his prior association with me as a caddy at the defunct South Shore Country Club in Chicago. His name was David.

I liked David and his friend Lucian, even though I did not really identify with their "born-again" form of Christianity. During my freshman year, I got into the habit of joining them to study at night, but they weren't my drinking buddies on the nights when I wasn't studying, which, to be perfectly honest, were all too frequent. It was just as well, I thought, because I did not really share their passion for "religion," which is what I presumed their faith to be, at the time.

Still, I was intrigued by them, and we often engaged in spiritual discussions that sometimes took the form of debates. With hindsight, I'd have to admit that sometimes the debates we had were as much sport for me as a reflection of genuine spiritual hunger. I liked those guys, but I enjoyed being "clever," and it is so easy to quote things out of context and to contort their meanings. Although it wasn't the ideal context for spiritual development, I can see now that God was at work back then, and I can warn you that the atheists who write today to convince you of their point of view may well be making sport of you as they invite you into their barren spiritual condition. As they say, misery loves company, even spiritual misery, I surmise. Our response to the invitation that they extend should emulate that of my friends—sincere engagement and prayers for their enlightenment. Over time, we may win them over, or at least develop more empathy for their spiritual condition and a better understanding of the root causes of their painful separation from God.[3]

In addition to the obvious differences with respect to beer drinking and study habits, these Christian men exhibited a genuine passion for leading a spiritual life that clearly set them apart from most of the people I lived with at the time. Their faith was a part of their daily experience. But that is not what intrigued me the most about them, either.

What intrigued me the most about them was that they had an indescribable light in their eyes that seemed to set them apart from just about every other person I had ever met or seen, except certain other born-again Christians or certain devout spiritual leaders from some other religious denominations. Although I did not realize it at the time, and I did not spend enough time with them to deepen my relationship with them enough to share in their brand of faith, I now know that the fire in their eyes was the radiant light of Christ that is promised in many, many places in the Bible, and referenced in the Scripture at the beginning of this chapter.

Would you like to have that kind of radiance in your life? As I grew older and I recognized that something was missing—despite all of my obvious blessings—I sure longed for it. But for a long time, I looked everywhere else but where I might actually find it. The Bible tells us that "Those who look to God are radiant" (Psalms 34:5). I could have saved myself a lot of time and spiritual anxiety, manifested as spiritual emptiness, had I started there.

DISCUSSION/STUDY QUESTIONS FOR CHAPTER TWO

1. What does the Bible tell us about God's willingness to relate to human beings?

2. How do the stories about the struggles of the faithful, even titans of faith like Abraham, Moses and David – inform our faith lives? What do they suggest about the pathway to faith?

3. We all take risks in search of reward, for example in our careers or with our investments. What types of risks are you willing to take in your faith life? What risks won't you take? What type of reward do you expect, given the risks you are willing to take?

4. Reflecting on your past, have you met people of deep faith that made you wish you had what they did? Did you ask how they came to that faith? What do you think they would tell you? Can you still ask?

5. How does your childhood and the religious guidance that you received, if any, reflect in your faith life today? Do you still practice the religion of your childhood? Why or why not?

6. Are you more or less trusting of God than you were as a child? Why or why not?

CHAPTER THREE

FROM THEN TO NOW

THE HEAVENS DECLARE THE GLORY OF GOD; THE SKIES PROCLAIM THE WORK OF HIS HANDS. (PSALMS 19:1)

In the prior chapter, I covered nearly half my existence, but I haven't given you even a glimmer of the guy who is writing for you now, so I hope with this chapter to get you quickly from then to now, or nearly now, anyway. I may also have some misconceptions to clear up, so I will jump right into one of those.

First, I have always believed in God. I've always believed in God the Creator because it seemed illogical to do otherwise. Reflecting on a spectacular sunrise that I once saw while standing at the top of a crater in Hawaii—a sunrise that was a spiritual experience for all who were there—I cannot imagine how anybody could believe that the wonderful world in which we live in is the result of pure chance playing out over time. After all, what are the odds of something this ordered and spectacular being totally random?

If you saw a car driving down the street and somebody suggested it was a chance collection of atoms and molecules that assembled themselves into that shape over time, wouldn't you consider that suggestion utterly ridiculous? If the chances of that are so low, what are the chances that the designers and builders of that car are a random occurrence? Lower still, it would seem.[4] Although this argument does not fit the "if A then B" construction that we were all taught in school, it does have some intuitive appeal, doesn't it?

But faith in God is not only intuitive, it is rational. In our lifetimes it is likely that we will never know enough to prove or disprove the existence of God, so it comes down to what we want to believe and the consequences of that choice. If we believe there is no God, and God exists, we risk getting eternity wrong. On the other hand, if we choose to believe in God and at the end of time it happens we were wrong, what will have been lost by our pursuing the hope, redemption, and love that the Bible promises He has to offer? There is only one rational choice. Accordingly, I do not understand how someone could choose atheism.

But, I acknowledge the unknown; so, at one level, I understand agnosticism, which literally means "without knowledge." Agnosticism seems to come from a different place than atheism and it seems to takes more forms, including, in my case, the form of someone raised Catholic and attending church every week. No, I never considered myself agnostic, but if Christ is who He claimed to be (and there is strong evidence that He is)[5] and the Bible is not just a collection of interesting stories handed down through time, then I, with my focus on my family, my career, and me—and not much else really—at a minimum, had a problem of priorities that manifested itself no differently than agnosticism, except for about an hour on Sundays. If I had truly received Christ, then my type of "faith" was impossible.

Reflecting the limitations of what we can truly know, the history of Christian faith includes some arguments among its adherents. Some of these have given rise to the different Christian denominations and churches. One of those arguments is about "faith" versus "works" as regards the question of salvation. It is an important argument, so it is important that you know where I stand. I believe that salvation comes to us through faith. But does my belief that salvation comes through faith imply that the concerns I expressed in the prior paragraph about the lack of outward manifestations of my faith were heedless? I sincerely believe that the answer is "no." I was right to be worried about my spiritual condition.

When we reach out to God in faith, He changes us, and when we become followers of Jesus that creates certain obligations. If we aren't responding to those obligations, then we are right to be worried about the authenticity of our faith. We could be treating faith in God like a talisman that allows us to continue to live self-centered lives, even though that is quite contrary to the message of the Bible. Or worse, we could be treating God's grace like something we can invoke merely by asking for it, so that we can go on living the way we intend, rather than as He instructs. At best, this may be a form of paganism or agnosticism; perhaps sacrilege, at worst.

The message of the Bible is that faith is a gift of God, freely given, not taken but received, and that real faith evidences itself in true believers. In other words, real faith "works."

Let me give you an example from my childhood of a story that illustrates the contrary position, which seems to take God's grace for granted. When I was little, I was with a friend in the corner drug store. When we left the store, he started munching on a candy bar that he had stolen while we were in there. I was shocked that he took it, and I was scared that I might be implicated, but what truly struck me was that he was completely comfortable with his actions. He did not seemed concerned about consequences of ANY kind! Then he told me the source of his comfort. "Stealing the candy bar was okay," he said, because he could "confess it on Saturday."

Unfortunately, many of us, recognizing the truth that it is through faith we are saved, may adopt an attitude of complacency not dissimilar to his. We may assume that since our sins are forgiven, we need not concern ourselves much about changing our actions. The risk to us is that the result of our complacency may be that our faith may be no more deeply developed than the faith of my childhood friend in the grocery store.

The writer of James and other passages in the Bible suggest that if our deeds do not evidence it, we may not have faith at all![6] And if we do not have faith, we do not have grace. In that case, our salvation and our deeds are still linked through the authentic faith that not only gains us salvation, but also transforms our very personhood.

Regardless of where one stands on faith versus works, if our faith is merely a statement, then we risk losing out on something that is much more than that—something which we deeply desire. And the problem with deep, unsatisfied desires is that they may manifest themselves in many ways, some of them good, some not so good. Even seemingly "good" diversions like working hard and focusing on our careers can lead to separation from God, as I fear they did with me.

While recognizing that I have more than my share of faults, I always thought that, on balance, I had channeled myself reasonably productively. I went to graduate school after university; I held a couple of interesting positions with good companies, and I met and married a terrific lady, Sandy, when I was twenty-seven years old. In at least one way, she was very like me, very career oriented. So, while I focused on working hard and garnering some additional credentials to further my career, she did the same, earning a Master of Science in Communication degree from Northwestern University in the early years of our marriage, while working full time.

We did the other things that ambitious young couples do. We paid our debts, bought a house, had a child, bought a bigger house, pushed ourselves in our careers, formed a company at one point after Sandy had opted to stay home full time, had another child, raised our children, took them to church every week, saved and invested our money, moved to better career opportunities when they presented themselves to us, and generally continued to prosper.

We loved each other, we loved our kids, we made good money and, although we are not extravagant, we took vacations that many people could only dream about. By most measurement standards, we were doing very well. But, we both knew that despite love, increasing wealth, health, and prosperity, something seemed to be missing.

Some people argue that the yearning we feel for God is really just the remnant of an evolutionary gene that served some other purpose years and years ago. Although they may be right about the existence of the genetic marker, perhaps the purpose of it hasn't changed at all!

The Bible tells us that the world in which we live will NEVER be enough for us because of our inborn longing for God.[7] Deep down, perhaps at the genetic level, we want to experience God. We know that God exists, but, being thinking people, we have questions and concerns: If God is good, all-knowing, and all-powerful, why is the world so bad? Which religion is right? Organized religions have been responsible for some truly horrible acts. Some Christians seem so exclusive, if not downright nasty. Is being part of a religion a sign of weakness? The list of questions and doubts could go on and on. Every thinking person has had some such question at one point or another in his or her spiritual life.

So what do we do with all of these questions? Do we stop there? Do we say "I believe," because we're afraid that if we don't we will go to hell one day, but don't bother to change any other aspect of our lives? Do we get mad at God, because He won't visit or talk to us like He seems to have done with the patriarchs of old? Do we start to deny His existence, because he won't make everything right in the world? Do we go through the motions of someone who believes, hoping that some day we actually may feel that we do? Do we just quit, without confronting our doubts or doing much of anything at all?

As the pastor of the Iowa church that I visited while writing this section of the book said, if the brakes on our cars weren't working, would we ignore them? If we took the car someplace and they didn't fix the brakes correctly would we stop going to that place and simply leave things as they were? Of course we wouldn't. Our salvation is a heck of a lot more important than our brakes, so what should we do?

We all need to confront this problem; in my case, I got fed up. I got fed up because the spiritual aspect of my life was the ONE area of my life that just didn't seem to be working. Everything else in my life seemed good, but everything else just wasn't enough. Being a self-help junkie and, at the time, a big believer in self-determinism, I was frustrated that this one aspect of my life seemed out of my control. So, at about age thirty-nine, I challenged God, to the extent one can "challenge" the Almighty, to reveal Himself to me. But, thankfully, I took the responsibility to do my part as well.

The things that I did are the subject of most of this book, but the short list is this: I started practicing thankfulness, resulting in a little more humility, and causing me to appreciate more deeply than ever before that my life was already blessed in innumerable ways; I read the Bible from front to back (I actually followed a reading plan that went Old Testament, New Testament, Old Testament, New Testament...but I read it all the way through), and then I started reading it again; I made a deliberate effort to "be still" with more regularity; I learned a little bit that exercise called prayer that I had been doing weekly at church—or perhaps I should say "weakly"—and I learned to pray more effectively (which happened to be the way I had been taught all along). In short, I tried to be mindful of, and on the lookout for, God in my life.

Sometime well into my spiritual journey, Sandy and I joined another church that held to the same foundational beliefs of the other churches that we had attended throughout our lives, but that connected with us and our children very differently. And, very importantly, as a consequence of having joined that church, we came to more fully appreciate the concept of tithing.

The result of all of this was that I started really paying attention to God, what He had done, and what He was doing in my life; and I finally began to appreciate that He had been working to reveal Himself to me all along. I had been just too busy, for nearly forty years, to notice. If any of this sounds at all familiar to you, then maybe you are ready for a breakthrough. When you have that breakthrough, you won't have to wonder about whether God exists or is active in your life, because you will experience Him in such a way that YOU WILL KNOW.

DISCUSSION/STUDY QUESTIONS FOR CHAPTER THREE

1. Is your concept of God like that described in the opening paragraphs of this chapter – a Creator who started things spinning and now just watches? What are the foundations of your concept of God? Has the Bible influenced your concept at all? How does your concept of God compare to the God presented in the Bible?

2. How can the doctrine of salvation by faith lead to spiritual complacency? Do you think that you have become spiritually complacent? If so, how is that affecting other areas of your life?

3. Is organized religion sometimes an obstacle to faith? Can our generalizations about organized religion also be such an obstacle? How can you tell the difference between the two?

4. Are you upset with God or challenged to believe in His existence because He won't fix everything? If you have or had children, do you, or would you, fix everything for them?

CHAPTER FOUR

PRACTICE THANKFULNESS

PRAISE THE LORD, O MY SOUL, AND FORGET NOT ALL HIS BENEFITS.
(PSALMS 103:2)

I consider myself one of the luckiest people in the world. At one level I have always believed that, but I haven't always lived my life that way. Even today, I'm not always conscious of the many blessings in my life and, as a result, I'm not always deeply connected to God, the source of those blessings. Let me give you some examples.

As I mentioned, I was fortunate enough to attend one of the best college prep schools in the country. From there, I went on to the University of Michigan, on a full academic scholarship. Michigan is considered one of the finest educational institutions in the world. After that, I went on to graduate school at the University of Chicago, another fine institution, and I obtained an MBA. That education proved a good foundation for the working years that followed.

My career has taken me to many of the great cities of the world: Chicago, New York, San Francisco, London, Buenos Aires, Zurich, Milan, Tokyo, Dublin, Paris, and Hong Kong among them. As a result, I have been fortunate enough to have worked with some of the brightest and best-educated people on the planet.

FAITH AFTER FORTY

To be perfectly honest, at one point in my life I considered myself a self-made person. In my mind, I worked to earn the money to put myself through high school; I earned the scholarship that paid for my college education; I worked and borrowed to go to graduate school, and I worked long hours and obtained the additional credentials that gave me the employment opportunities I have described above. I am not one to boast, but I was proud of my accomplishments, and I felt like I had earned my good fortune. Although I was not an arrogant person, having considered it further, I can see how terribly ungracious it was for me to have considered my accomplishments to be my own successes, even if only a little bit.

I was born in the United States, the richest country in the world. I had two loving, healthy and hard-working parents. I never went hungry. I always went to school, and the teachers at those schools were nothing short of terrific. These are privileges that many in the world do not share.

My parents taught me the value of hard work; some children have no such example. They made it clear that I was going to attend one of the best college preparatory schools in the country and that they expected me to pay the tuition to do so. It was not negotiable, nor did it even enter my mind to contradict it. They sacrificed their time and comfort to make sure that we did the things necessary to prepare for and pay for that experience. Many children do not have that type of guidance.

My brothers and I caddied for two reasons: to help to pay for high school, and in the hopes of earning a scholarship to college. My oldest brother had accomplished both before they were objectives for me. Thank God for his good example. Who knows if I would have been as motivated to obtain the scholarship had he not done so? But the issue ran so much deeper than simple motivation. After all, do you ever really "earn" a scholarship? A scholarship is someone's money set aside to help someone else. I didn't earn the scholarship; I qualified for it and it was given to me. There's a big difference between earning and qualifying. To be honest, I don't think that I fully appreciated it at the time. In my mind, I knew the criteria for the scholarship, I was working to meet the criteria, and I pretty much expected that I'd get the scholarship. My only "plan B" was to join the ROTC if it did not work out. Thank God I was awarded, which is to say given, the Evans Scholarship. Perhaps needless to say, at some point I came to appreciate more fully the blessing of it.

While caddying, a member of the club took an interest in my brothers and me. His name was Ed. Maybe he was intrigued by the fact that four boys from the same family were working there at the same time, or perhaps he took an interest because he was Irish and we obviously were as well. Regardless, I was blessed in many ways for having known him. At some point, he offered me an internship with an actuarial consulting firm. In that context, I ended up working for Joe, who became a mentor in terms of work ethic and, ultimately, a very good friend. In addition, compared to other alternatives available to me at the time, the work was relatively lucrative. Finally, working there familiarized me at a very young age with a professional environment, which no doubt helped me later in my career.

Ed also sat on the board that awarded the Evans Scholarship. He may have directly influenced their decision to award the scholarship to me. Having since sat on the committee that awards the scholarship, I know full well that my brother's success in the program undoubtedly helped my case as an applicant.

Finally, when I was considering graduate school, Ed introduced me to a trustee of the University of Chicago, who may have influenced my later acceptance at that institution. I'll never really know for sure, but having considered it further, I think that I can reasonably conclude that my grades, test scores, and hustle were only part of the reason that I was admitted to the University of Chicago for graduate school.

As we practice thankfulness, we take a fresh perspective on our lives. We see the broader context for our accomplishments. Every promotion, every award, every advancement usually involves somebody else. Even if that somebody is only paying attention to us and recognizing our efforts, they're involved.

What if I had been born in a poor country or my parents had been killed in genocide or war? What if I had been sold into slavery, or I suffered from diseases or afflictions that in our society are virtually unknown? No matter how diligent, educated, or hardworking, my life would be very different.

We can start practicing thankfulness by making a list of the things we should be thankful for, then spending some time graciously contemplating that list. When I did this, I realized that God had richly blessed me, and that He had been very active in my life, but I was too busy trying to "make it all happen" on my own to fully appreciate His blessings. I thank God that I finally took the time to notice.

I am no longer proud of anything that I have accomplished; I am grateful for the many, many opportunities and all of the wonderful, nurturing people that I have had in my life.

Many self-help books will tell you that the practice of gratefulness is one of the more important aspects of a happy and fulfilling life, presumably because of all of the positive associations that the practice engenders. It seems to me much more than that. Gratefulness helps to destroy pride, and in doing so removes one of the obstacles that prevents us from enjoying real closeness to God.

DISCUSSION/STUDY QUESTIONS FOR CHAPTER FOUR

1. We may take pride in the idea that we are "self-made." Recall some of the significant accomplishments of your life and consider how others may have been involved in them. Could God have been working through those people to bless you?

2. How would your life be different if you lived among the poorest of the world's poor? Given the abundance of the planet, what is the source of their suffering and why does it persist?

3. What do you have to be thankful for that has absolutely nothing to do with your efforts? Why do you think you enjoy these blessings? Can you extend them to someone else?

CHAPTER FIVE

READ THE BIBLE

EVERY PART OF SCRIPTURE IS GOD-BREATHED AND USEFUL ONE WAY OR ANOTHER—SHOWING US TRUTH, EXPOSING OUR REBELLION, CORRECTING OUR MISTAKES, TRAINING US TO LIVE GOD'S WAY. THROUGH THE WORD WE ARE PUT TOGETHER AND SHAPED UP FOR THE TASKS GOD HAS FOR US.[8] (2 TIMOTHY 3:16)

Although I could never say it out loud (perhaps because I was afraid I'd be lost for having done so), about a decade ago, I was one of those people who thought God was just sort of "out there" and not terribly engaged in our world. If challenged, I would have to say that my belief was that the God described in the Bible seemed to defy reason and logic; or, in any case, it seemed that He stopped talking to us long ago. I was willing to believe that He set things in motion, but my sense was that now He was mostly watching us to see how we do with what He started. After all, how could the world be what it is today if God were actively involved in it? It just didn't seem possible.

Expressed or not, this notion is completely inconsistent with the Christian faith. It is almost astounding that someone who was born and raised Catholic, who was an altar boy for so many years, and who still went to church every Sunday could even consider such a thing possible. It shows how apathetic I had become in my faith. Technically speaking, I had become a Deist without even recognizing it; I still considered myself Catholic.

40

Practically speaking, I had become an agnostic, because, obviously, I did not know God.

One cannot believe the basic story of the Bible and believe that God is the distant being that I have described in the penultimate paragraph above. Thankfully, I set aside this belief long enough to read the Bible and, responding to my deep longing for God, I prayed for a miracle. In my case, though, the miracles began before I even began reading, with the receipt of a Bible on Christmas day in 1999.

As it is with many Christians, Christmas has always been special in our household. However, I'd have to admit that the focus in my household was more secular than sacred. Gifts given tended to be things like jewelry for my wife, art supplies or books for me and more toys than my daughter could ever really use. That year, although I bought some of the usual things for Sandy, I also bought her one gift that I had hoped would resonate more deeply with her, and that I felt was more in tune with the true spirit of the season. I bought her a study Bible. We owned other Bibles, and Sandy had not asked me to get her one, but it seemed like the perfect gift at the time.

Sandy unwrapped her present, and I could see that I had accomplished what I had hoped. It was very clear that the gift seemed special, if for no other reason because it was unlike anything that I had ever given her before. But her reaction to my gift was different than just surprise. There was something sublime in her reaction that I did not totally understand, until she handed me the last of my gifts. It, too, was a study Bible. Sandy, nearly eight months pregnant with our soon-to-be-born son, felt the same urge that I had, which was to try to make that Christmas different and special, and she arrived at the same idea about how to accomplish that objective.

Now, I probably have done a terrible job of relating this story in writing, but if you're like most people to whom we have told it, then you may have goose pimples right about now. You know God was at work that day.

If you feel anything at all, pay special attention to that feeling, because I think it is one way that God lets you know He is paying attention to you, and that He wants to deepen His relationship with you. Search for that feeling again and again in your life. You will be shocked by how often you find it, and how closely it mirrors your circumstances.

God subtly lets us know that He is near. Having an awareness of God helps us to feel His presence. Reading the Scriptures helps us to develop that awareness, because we can see how—and how consistently—God has revealed Himself to His people throughout time.

As you might expect, Sandy and I talk about nearly everything. Married couples do that. But, neither one of us had mentioned to the other the unsatisfied longing for God that, it turns out, we were both experiencing at the same time. I can only conjecture that, being somewhat traditional in our approach to religion or belief, we each struggled silently and stoically, hoping that it would go away. Instead, God moved us off the dime toward growing spiritually through the inspiration for these reciprocal Bible presents. That day, I resolved to read the entire Bible in the year that I turned forty, and it is safe to say that, while it has had its ups and downs, my life has never been quite the same since.

I sincerely believe that you cannot read The Holy Bible and come out the same person who started reading it. Scripture is just too powerful. That is why the Bible has lasted thousands of years, that is why it is still relevant today, and that is why, in my mind, reading the Bible is THE essential spiritual discipline if you seek a strong relationship with God.

I believe that if you are atheist when you start reading it, you may believe when you finish; if you are agnostic, you may become Christian, and if you are Christian, you will, without question, deepen your relationship with the Trinity: the Father, the Son, and the Holy Spirit. Of course, if you re-read it, then I believe that you will keep moving along the continuum. If spiritual motivations are not enough, consider that the Bible is history, epic literature, and the best-selling book ever. We should read it for literary reasons alone.

If I believe all of these things about reading the Bible, then why didn't I make it the subject of the earlier chapter? There are a several reasons.

First, while it can be comfortably done in less than a year, reading the Bible is no easy task. The Bible was written over many centuries, in different periods of history, and in different languages reflecting different cultures. We have to do a lot of reading and study in order to develop even a modicum of appreciation for what it says. It helps to buy a good study Bible and to read all of the footnotes in it in order to have even a basic understanding of the cultural context and subtleties of the text.

We own several different translations, each of which offers the additional insight that alternative translations can bring, and I have since learned that there are editions of the Bible that include more than one translation side-by-side.

Second, there are advantages to practicing gratefulness before we begin our Bible study. In some ways, gratefulness conditions us for the task of reading. Think of it this way: if you were really out of shape, you wouldn't start lifting weights without doing at least a little conditioning in advance. If you did not do that pre-conditioning, you'd probably hurt yourself and quit your exercise program. Conditioning ourselves to receive God's Word by practicing gratefulness enhances our chances of success. Also, since reading the entire Bible will likely take months, we are well served to practice something that gives more immediate results as we start down the road to a deeper faith. Gratefulness is that something.

Finally, the practice of gratefulness helps to open us up to the idea that God has been working in our lives all along, thus empowering us to ask Him to help us get through the exercise of reading the Bible with understanding. This is very important; because the Bible warns against leaning on our own understanding. We really do need the Holy Spirit to open up our eyes and our hearts to His Word.

Reading the entire Bible is an incredibly important exercise on the road to stronger faith, so please do not let prior attempts at reading the Bible, being "too busy," or the difficulty of the task sway you from getting through the entire Bible, from the front cover to the back cover. Also, do not let the contents of some of the stories, strange though they may seem, stop your progress.

After discussing the benefits of reading the Bible with someone close to me, I recall him responding that he had read the entire Bible when he was ten or eleven years old. He rolled his eyes and said something to the effect of "Geez, what kinds of stories are those? People killing one another, girls sleeping with their father, some of that stuff is sick, really sick." Yes, as the pastor in our church said on the Sunday before I began writing this chapter, the Bible is, indeed, full of stories about seriously flawed people: "priests, prophets, poets, and prostitutes—and even some people whose names don't begin with 'p.'"[9] Yes, there are a number of very strange stories, which reflect some of the atrocities that man is capable of, but there is a context for those stories that begins with the first chapter of Genesis and ends at the last chapter of Revelation. It is unlikely that a ten- or eleven-year-old, no matter how bright, would be able to grasp that context.

It is very important for us to approach the Bible with an open and receptive mind. After all, can anyone really speak to us when we're not ready to listen? Even without the barriers of centuries of change, things lost in translation, and things handed down orally from generation to generation, we fail to relate well to one another when we don't truly listen and try to first accept and understand what we hear. So, if we open our Bibles convinced that we will be wasting our time, we probably will be wasting our time.

Instead, let's try to relate what the Bible says to what we already believe. This helps us to be open to its message and to develop a better understanding of what the writers were trying to convey. After all, we know a lot more today about the earth and the stars than the writers did. Even though they were God-inspired, men ultimately put the words on the page. Being careful not to suggest that the Bible is anything short of the truth, and being careful not to add or take away from Scripture, it seems reasonable that God spoke to men and women in the context of their times and in a language they could understand. We need to bridge the gap between us and those men and women, and allow Him to speak to us today through what they wrote then.

To illustrate what I have in mind, I'm going to make a very specific suggestion to get you started. When you read the creation account, even if you don't believe it, consider how it might fit within your current understanding. You may find yourself intrigued by how you can reconcile what you read with your existing beliefs and knowledge. For example, scientists say that there was a "big bang." The Bible says "God spoke." Those could be the same. Science suggests that swirling balls of gas formed into planets. The Bible says "Now the earth was formless and empty" (Genesis 1:2). Those could be the same. Evolution suggests that fish and birds preceded man. The Bible account suggests they did as well. That is truly remarkable, considering when it was written. Science says that all of this took billions of years; the Bible says that it happened in six days. But what is a day to an infinite Being?

Do you see how remaining open to the fundamental truths of Scripture does not require us to dismiss what we think we have learned about the origins of man and our universe since these things were written down? I am not suggesting that the Bible says that we evolved, nor am I saying that every word of the Bible will connect literally with your current understanding; I am only saying that you may be surprised by how much of what we believe today is not necessarily inconsistent with something written thousands of years ago, long before we had the scientific discoveries that support our current understanding of the world, as long as we approach the Bible with sincerity and we don't take things too literally. That is miraculous, when you think about it. As we look for these potential miracles of understanding, instead of reading literally or cynically, we may start to hear God speaking to us, even if allegorically.

Some people attempt to discredit the accounts of the Bible by likening them to the myths of pagan contemporaries or predecessors of the Biblical writers. Isn't it possible that God was trying to speak to those people, too—in ways that they could understand—and that this is the reason for the similarities? When we try to teach somebody something, don't we try to adapt the material to something that the person conceptually understands? Why would we expect God to do otherwise? We need to open our minds to the idea that it may be so, rather than automatically discredit the Biblical accounts because of such similarities. Also, we need to remember as we read that the Bible was unique in at least one very important way: the assumption of one, sovereign God. This consequential difference cannot be ignored.

As a final example, we have to be careful not to impute human motives to God when we read stories of invasion and war at God's bidding. Everything has a context. We must always remember that a holy God abhors sin. Such stories, reflecting the consequences of sin given the very nature of God, help to set the stage for the need for some God-given reconciliation and the arrival of Jesus Christ.

The Bible is an amazing story, written over centuries, by people who didn't know each other, yet who managed to write one, cohesive story. What motivated these people to write? When reading the Old Testament, it is clear that life often was not easy for the people who took the time to write down those stories and prophecies. Yet they wrote anyway. The New Testament was written by people who were intelligent and literate, and who knew that they would probably be killed for preaching the resurrection of Jesus. Still, they did so.

What gave these people the courage, the wisdom and the will to write? The ruling powers of government and the religious leaders of the day certainly did not want the story of the resurrection of Christ to get around. They crucified the man—the worst death imaginable—because they wanted to put down once and for all the insurrection they thought His movement could bring. They posted a guard at the tomb, because they did not want anyone to secret away the body and give credence to Jesus' predicted resurrection.

And their intimidation worked for a time. After His death, Jesus' followers scattered and hid. The Bible tells us that they locked themselves away in a room. Yet these people, who by

48

their own account were frightened into hiding, suddenly became emboldened to proclaim the resurrection of Jesus. What power on earth could have caused that to happen?

We often overlook the fact that the great heroes of the Bible, just like us, had their moments of doubts and fears. Considering the hostile circumstances they endured, their doubts and fears were probably much greater than our own. Somehow they overcame them. They persisted. Unfortunately, because we are reading with the benefit of hindsight, we might overlook the courage that it took for them to persist in their faith. We have much to learn from their stories.

As you read, put yourself into the stories. Which character is most like you? How does that character get over his or her doubts and fears about God? The heroes of the Bible teach us to be patient in our faith, to wait on God, and to listen carefully for how He might lead us. Reading their stories strengthens us to do this and attunes us to God so we are ready to respond when He calls.

One more thing about reading the Bible: while you're reading, not only should you pray for a miracle, but you should expect one. In doing so, you will be emulating the faith of those heroes of the Bible. When we wait for God, align our wills with His, and expect a miracle, we may just get one. However, as my wife Sandy reminded me to say after reading this passage, we need to recognize that miracles can be small, daily happenings, not just things grandiose. The more finely attuned we are to the circumstances of our lives, the more likely we are to discover God's miracles.

As you might have guessed by now, when I decided to read the Bible I was not much more than an agnostic in Christian clothing. I did not expect any miracles. Then God started serving them up to me, even before my journey through the Bible officially began, with the receipt of the Bible that Christmas from my wife, Sandy. As I mentioned, I vowed to read the Bible cover to cover, and in the five or six months that followed I did exactly that. And then my life started to change, rapidly and for the better.

Some changes were quite tangible. For example, I was promoted and transferred to an affiliated company in my home town. For Sandy and me, this literally was an answer to a prayer. But more importantly, and as suggested in the quote at the beginning of this chapter, I started to change. Even if my circumstances had not changed, or if they had changed for the worse, God's Word was shaping me up for things that would come later—like writing this book, for instance. It is a welcome change that brings meaning and purpose to life in a way that a better job, more money, positive mental imaging, affirmations, or anything else that I could obtain or do never could.

I hope and pray that your journey through the Bible will do the same for you. Start reading the Bible now. You won't regret it. And if you really want to make some progress, join a Bible study. You'll be surprised at how much there is to learn from fellow seekers and believers.

DISCUSSION/STUDY QUESTIONS FOR CHAPTER FIVE

1. Most people of faith trace the roots of their belief back to some fundamental document. Have you read the entirety of the scriptures that underlie your faith?

2. What does the Bible tell us about the character of God? What do you believe? How and why do they differ? If you believe some parts of Scripture, but not others, how can you be sure about the foundations of your faith?

3. Does the Bible have to be literally true in order to be valid? Why or why not? Jesus often spoke in illustrative parables that contained great underlying moral and religious truths. Do you think that he would defend the Bible as literal truth?

4. If one believes in evolution, does that imply that the Bible must be false? Why do some people frame science and faith as an "either...or" debate?

5. Who do you identify most with in the Bible? Which person would you like to be? How could you become more like him or her?

CHAPTER SIX

PRAY CONSTANTLY

ONE DAY JESUS WAS PRAYING IN A CERTAIN PLACE. WHEN HE FINISHED, ONE OF HIS DISCIPLES SAID TO HIM, "LORD, TEACH US TO PRAY, JUST AS JOHN TAUGHT HIS DISCIPLES." HE SAID TO THEM... (LUKE 11:1-2A)

Praying seems to come naturally to some people. I have participated in Bible study groups with other Christians and I have been astounded at their ability to pray—especially in their ability to pray extemporaneously and aloud. Unfortunately for me, I was not one of those people particularly adept at prayer, spoken or otherwise. Except for services on Sunday, I rarely prayed, and when I did, I usually recited rote prayers in my head. To be perfectly honest, I really didn't expect much, if anything, to come of my prayers, so I did not put too much into them. What I have come to discover is that, like most things in life, what you put into prayer often dictates what you get out of it.

As I started immersing myself in the Bible, one thing that became clear is that prayer is the way by which people establish an open connection to God. What also seemed clear, though, was that I was not praying nearly enough, and/or I must have been going about it all wrong, because it did not seem worth even the little bit of time I was giving it. So, as is typical for me, I gave myself an ultimatum. Either I wasn't going to bother with praying and I would channel my energy elsewhere, or I would continue to pray but figure out what I was doing wrong. Thankfully, I chose the latter course.

In typical "figure it out for myself" fashion, I bought a few books about prayer. I bought four or five books, actually, so I will try to summarize some of them for you in the context of my own experience in order to encourage you to explore the topic further. I recommend that you consider purchasing the books mentioned, but my hope is that this quick summary can get you started on the journey to more effective prayer. In either case, I am certain you will get there faster than I did.

First, I bought a prayer book "for today's Catholic" that offered up various forms of prayer—for the seasons of the year, for special feasts from the liturgical calendar and for people, occasions, and special needs. It contains some really beautiful prayers, but reading from the book only reinforced for me that I did not know how to pray, and reading prayers composed by someone else did not seem to make me any better at it.

Later, I read a book about an "ancient Christian prayer form" called "centering prayer" in a book by the same name, authored by M. Basil Pennington.[10] As soon as I started reading, I knew I was on to something, because the introduction to this book resonated with me. It expressly recognizes that prayer requires us to get in touch with ourselves and our experiences. It reinforces the idea that prayer has to come from deep within us, in light of what is going on in our lives. The book helped me to understand that without faith and without the Holy Spirit, prayer may be a waste of time, but with faith and with the Holy Spirit we can meet the God of the Bible, the one who "made man to be his intimate friend." It helped me to find the silence that we all, as Pennington states, "possess for the sake of delicate listening." Most importantly, it illuminated the idea of using prayer to "purely and simply seek God, without any expectations."

Seek God without any expectations. Prior to reading the book, it had never occurred to me to do anything without expecting some sort of result. It was natural for me to want to do things with the ambition of accomplishing something, rather than simply to do them. Pennington pointed out that expectations involve seeking something for ourselves, which undermines "the very essence of this prayer, which is a total, pure, seeking of God." In doing this, in focusing only on seeking God, we remove the barrier of our self from prayer and we experience what is promised in the Bible: "Come near to God and He will come near to you" (James 4:8). As my daughter Courtney's confirmation mentor asked her about this particular verse, "How cool is that?"

The book does a terrific job of exhorting us to make time for God—literally to put that time on our "to-do" lists. It also helps us to put such lists in perspective. When was the last time your to-do list said "spend some time with God"? I know that mine never did. Yet, at the end of the day, that is what prayer really is, time spent seeking and being with God. And the Bible promises that if we seek God, we will find Him. Making time for God is a terrific step in the right direction.

Finally, the book briefly touches on a form of prayer called *lectio divina* or "divine reading." I was piqued enough by what the author wrote to buy another book on the subject. My thought was that since I was reading the Bible anyway, this might be a way to infuse the exercise with more meaning. The book that I read, which I recommend to you, is *The Word is Very Near You,* by Martin L. Smith.[11]

Smith begins by pointing out that the desire we have for God, which causes us to read such books, is a result of us responding to God's initiative, not the other way around. For me, this was a very important insight. It was much easier for me to take my prayer life more seriously when I recognized that it was God's reaching out to me in the first place that caused me to want to pray. It helped me to trust that the time I would invest in the process would bear fruit.

The second chapter of the book really struck a chord. Smith begins with an intuitive definition of prayer: "Prayer is a conversation with God." But, he insightfully instructs that this "standard definition of prayer masks all sorts of misgivings and confusion about what kind of conversation (prayer) is." I assure you that, in the pages to follow, he writes something which will resonate with you personally: for example, how our prayers don't seem to get answered or how our prayers seem to get interrupted by the 'static' of random thoughts." However, as Smith causes us to nod our heads in agreement to these things, he offers that "our insistence that there is something wrong with the way we pray is a thin veil for RESENTMENT (emphasis added) of a God whom we have experienced as a passive partner in prayer." Wow, I didn't see that coming! With hindsight, though, I have to admit that is exactly what was undermining my own attempts at prayer; I really didn't believe God was listening.

Thankfully, Smith offers that such thoughts, "blasphemous and irreligious" as they seem, "are true allies in the movement of growth and conversion." He notes that God is using our anger to shake us out of our acceptance of mediocrity in our relationship with Him. For me, one of the key insights of the book is the fundamental problem of the concept of prayer as a conversation with God: we naturally assume that WE are the ones initiating the conversation. As we see in story after story, this is inconsistent with the God of the Bible, who initiates all the time.

It helps to start thinking about prayer as "continuing a conversation which God has begun." It is a bit harder to find God absent from our prayer life, or our life in general, when we adopt this perspective. The author challenges us to see prayer differently: "What if God does not demand prayer as much as gives prayer? What if prayer is a means of God nourishing, healing, converting us? Suppose prayer is primarily allowing us to be loved, addressed, and claimed by God?" Now that is motivation enough for just about anybody.

Maybe all of my book reading was a good idea, because I learned how to look at the Scriptures as God making the first move to talk to us. It helped me to read more carefully, to at times turn off my seemingly insatiable curiosity or desire for reckoning, and to allow the Scriptures to do more of the talking. My Bible reading became less of a "mission" and more of a joy. The stories seemed to take on more meaning and more familiarity, leading to a much more personal encounter with God.

We encounter Jesus in meditative prayer because "The practice of meditative prayer is based on the fundamental

Christian belief that Christ is the Word of God, God's self-expression." As Martin Smith goes on to say, "In prayer, we expose ourselves to God's love in Christ, and we allow ourselves to experience it. Without this actual experience, the love of Christ remains a mere concept, an idea."

The Bible is full of encounters with God. The Bible is full of prayers. If we ever find ourselves unable to pray, we can simply open the Bible. We can turn almost anywhere in its pages and ask ourselves "How does this mirror what's going on in my life? How might this apply to me?" You will be astounded at the associations that you can make. Those associations are God talking to you in prayer.

Is something bothering you? Open up to Psalms and you'll find a way to complain to God. Complaining may not change anything, but complaining through the Scriptures may help to alter your perspective. Alternatively, you may find yourself or your circumstances somewhere else in the Bible. Dwell on those passages and let them inform your conversation with God. But remember, conversation is a two-way street; you will be surprised by how much you grow by simply listening.

Being a natural reader, it was easy for me to read the Bible for half an hour a day. And it became easy for me to spot the circumstances of my life that mirrored those of the people in the stories in the Bible. A pattern seemed to emerge. I found that the primary differences between my situation and the situations of the people I found in the Bible were (1) my circumstances were not even close to being as bad as their circumstances were, and (2) God sometimes seemed to take His time helping them, even when they were doing exactly what He told them to do. So, characteristically, I sought out a book about what I perceived as this problem of God being too slow. The book I found was *When God Takes Too Long*, by Joseph Bentz.[12]

This book is full of principles for waiting on God. I won't list them; they're right there in the table of contents of the book. But for me the key insight of the book is this: God's timing is not our timing, and God's plan for our life may have His eternal perspective. Pointing us to Scripture, the author reminds us that "The work God begins in me may be completed by other people. The work began in other people may be completed in me." This knowledge can help us to be more patient with the unfolding of God's intentions.

The author notes that we tend to think of God's plan for us in terms of ourselves, but what may seem inconsequential during OUR time may be more important OVER time. The book relates many instances of this in the Bible, but the one that really resonated with me—in fact, I was shocked when I encountered it during my own Bible study—was the story of Moses.

Most people remember that Moses led the Israelites out of Egypt, and that he was instrumental in God's miracles along the way. What I had forgotten from my youth, or perhaps never really knew, was that after leading the Israelites through the desert for forty years, Moses never got to enter the Promised Land. Did you remember that part of the story? After forty years of leading, shepherding, and wandering, Moses never got to enter the Promised Land!

Clearly, God had great plans for Moses. Today, Moses is revered by many of the world's great religions; and, as the Bible says at the end of Deuteronomy, "since then, no prophet has risen in Israel like Moses, whom the LORD knew face to face" (Deuteronomy 34:10). Still, Moses' work on earth was not completed by Moses; Joshua was the person who took the Israelites across the Jordan and into the Promised Land. And God had told Moses, in advance, that was how it was going to be. Despite that, Moses did not get caught up in his own ambitions for his life. Moses submitted to God and was happy to be part of His plan. Bentz reminds us that this is what we need to do and, when we do this, our lives become more meaningful and less burdened by expectations that have nothing to do with God's plans for us.

So, what does all of this stuff in the last few paragraphs have to do with prayer? What I found when I started approaching God in prayer without expectations, and when I began to recognize that God's plan for me might be different than my own, was that praying became easier and my prayers became more effective. I also found that the one of the prayers that I had reduced to little more than rote recitation on a weekly basis suddenly became infused with meaning.

Referring to the Scripture at the beginning of this chapter, when Jesus' disciples asked Him how to pray, He taught them the Lord' Prayer, sometimes referred to as the "Our Father." This was one of the prayers that I said routinely, at least every Sunday, which had lost its efficacy for me. Somehow, I had overlooked the fact that Jesus himself taught us this prayer, and that it is so foundational that every Christian church teaches it to its people. The verse linking prayer and God's timing is found in this prayer: "Thy will be done."

I finally appreciated that our job is to try to discern what God's will is, to align ourselves with the role God wants us to play, and to surrender our own ambitions to His higher calling. If we do that, our prayers will be productive, and our lives will be more in tune with God's great plan for us—a plan which will not manifest itself entirely while we are here on earth.

To extend some encouragement to you about your own prayer life, I will offer that I have become a big believer in prayer. At this point in my life, I even understand and can identify with the biblical exhortation to pray constantly. I pray much more frequently now, and I believe those prayers have efficacy. My prayer for you is that what worked for me will work for you, and that your prayer life will enhance—no, transform—your faith.

DISCUSSION/STUDY QUESTIONS FOR CHAPTER SIX

1. Does it change your prayer life to think of prayer as having been initiated by God? In what ways?

2. What is your approach to prayer? Is it always the same? How do you think you could change it to become more attuned to God?

3. How can you practice seeking God "without any expectations?" What do you think would happen as a result?

4. What do you think you might hear if you offered to do anything that God might ask of you? If you thought that you heard a clear answer, would you be willing to do it?

5. What does it mean to "wait on God?" Is such waiting a passive activity? In what other areas of your life are you content to simply wait? Does the fact that you may never in your lifetime know God's plan for you alter your view of how you should wait?

6. In various places in the Bible we are told to feed the poor and to care for the needy, such as widows, orphans, the crippled and the lame. In the absence of hearing more specific instructions from God, how might you use the Bible to discern God's will for you?

CHAPTER SEVEN

GIVE GENEROUSLY

THEN ABRAHAM GAVE HIM A TENTH OF EVERYTHING. (GENESIS 14:20)

As indicated in the quotation above, the concept of tithing has been around since Genesis. Unfortunately, it gets little mention in the New Testament and, perhaps as a result, seems like it has become outdated. The few specific references to tithing to be found in the New Testament relate to Jesus rebuking the Pharisees for doing it while at the same time treating others badly, or instances of the Pharisees lording their tithing over the less fortunate. These references do not speak specifically to the practice of tithing, and they do not convey Jesus' view of tithing, so much as they seem to convey His views on hypocrisy and condescension.

Moving to the present time, people of the modern world have ample reasons to be deeply suspicious of parting with their money in the interest of what some may deem as charitable causes. Politicians see the way forward to a more compassionate society funded by more taxes, so that the government can "take care" of other people. But we have legitimate concerns about the inefficient bureaucracy that we are entrusting with our money. In addition to the issue of the efficiency of those wealth transfers, we have reasonable cause to be suspicious of the motives behind them.

Cynical though it may seem, it is sometimes hard not to conclude that the motivation behind political speeches may be their interest in having people beholding to them in order to reinforce their elected positions, or that they may be pandering to one group of people in order to get their vote, using another group's money to do so. Neither of these possibilities inspires us to want to pay higher taxes for their stated charitable intentions. Those concerns aside, we may suspect that in many cases such transfer payments do not really benefit the people who receive them, but instead create a culture of dependency that does not ultimately meet their needs.

But our concerns do not stop with politicians. We see televangelists living lives of extravagance and preaching "prosperity Christianity" to people who often are not prosperous, asking for money in order to help spread their message. Once again, their lives and their exhortations may seem contrary to one another.

We see churches running deficits, shutting down their facilities and selling off their assets, with the money raised from these activities used to settle lawsuits resulting from cover-ups of notorious crimes. In a sense, the cover-ups were worse than the crimes themselves, because they institutionalized the aberrant behavior of the individuals. The leaders of these institutions assure us that our present donations are not being used in those settlements, but such assurances seem disingenuous. We know that one of the fundamental attributes of money is that it is fungible. In this respect, suggestions that our donations are not in some way funding these settlements seem contrary to the very nature of currency.

Considering all of this, it would not be hard for us to conclude that in many instances requests for our money should be ignored. We can be better stewards of capital ourselves.

Throughout my life, I was always taught that it is important to share; so I have always given to charity and I have always given to the churches I have attended. However, if truth be told, at some point in my life the paragraphs above did a reasonable job of summarizing where I had gotten on the concept of charitable giving. I believed that tithing was an Old Testament concept developed in an era of lower taxation. I believed that many of the institutions seeking "my" money would not use it wisely. I believed that I could do a better job of giving on my own. Unfortunately, I was erratic in this, and I usually found myself doling out a lot of money at the end of the year as I was forecasting my tax return, often realizing that my giving, although perhaps nominally high, was not terribly high compared to my income level. Thankfully, I read a book that helped to give me better perspective on the whole matter of giving: *The Treasure Principle*, by Randy Alcorn.[13]

At one level, tithing really is an Old Testament concept. Plug the word "tithe" into Bible software, and you get results that suggest the first paragraph of this chapter is right on the money. But, does the fact that tithing is an Old Testament concept imply that it is somehow invalidated by the New Testament? Of course not and, indeed, far from it.

Firstly, the Old and New Testaments are all part of the same story. One book does not supersede or invalidate the other. Secondly, the New Testament is primarily about the life of Jesus

Christ and the growth of the early church. Although His motivation may have been simply to show us our need for salvation, one thing that is clear is Jesus came to earth to raise the bar for us. For example, it is no longer enough for us to love each other; we need to love our enemies as much as we love ourselves. Consider that when the rich man asked Jesus what he needed to do to enter heaven, Jesus told him to sell his possessions, give the proceeds to the poor, and follow him.[14]

Although He did not use the word "tithe" as an exhortation to do it, Jesus talked a lot about money. Most of what He had to say revolved around the theme that having too much of it may be an obstacle to our relationship with God. This is because we are material beings and, as a result, we tend to focus on the material. That focus is the essence of the problem.

The Treasure Principle is based on a verse found in the New Testament: "Where your treasure is, there your heart will be also" (Matthew 6:21). In his book, Alcorn does a remarkably good job of reminding us that everything on earth belongs to God; we are just stewards of what He has given us. Importantly, he uses the New Testament and Jesus' own words to point out that how we steward the resources given to us will determine our reward in heaven.[15] That concept is worth repeating, because it is very important: *The Bible suggests that how well we steward the resources given to us on earth will determine our reward in heaven.* This implies that the stakes of our stewardship are very, very high.

Alcorn reminds us of our responsibility for each other and, most especially, he reminds those of us blessed with material abundance of the need to give generously.[16] For those with plenty of surplus, this may imply far more than the traditional ten percent of income that the word "tithe" may suggest. As Jesus intimates in the story of the poor woman giving two coins worth a fraction of a penny to the collection box,[17] it is not the absolute level of our giving that matters, it is whether we are giving until we feel joy, which may hurt a bit, at first. "Calling his disciples to him, Jesus said, 'Truly, I tell you, this poor widow has put more into the treasury than all the others. They all gave out of their wealth; but she, out of her poverty, put in everything—all that she had to live on'" (Mark 12:43-44).

Fairly recently, I read a quote attributed to a billionaire, a seemingly terrific fellow who is one of the truly great stewards of capital. Upon donating a significant part of his fortune to charity, he was reported to have remarked that he had thus secured his place in heaven. Although I suspect that he made the remark in jest, the premises of the statement still may be worth considering.

Of course, we cannot buy our way into heaven. Also, the Bible urges us not to wait until the end of our lives to share God's blessings. Read Jesus' parables about the rich man and a man named Lazarus (Luke 16:19-31) or another parable known as the "parable of the rich fool" (Luke 12:13-21) and consider the message of those stories. God wants to prosper us in every way, but the Bible makes clear that our prosperity is not primarily about how much money we have. Also, no matter how we choose to define "prosperity," prosperity and material excess are very different things. But I know from personal experience that the allure of accumulating money is very strong.

This is not to suggest that God is against capitalism or prosperity. History proves that capitalism is undoubtedly superior to other economic systems in creating prosperity, and in that sense capitalism is intrinsically good. Despite this, pundits are suggesting that the current global capital markets crisis could portend the final repudiation of capitalism. Capitalism is not the cause of the current economic upheaval; it more likely resulted from a pervasive lack of stewardship and such human attributes as pride, materialism and greed.[18] Capitalism actually helped to create the wealth that is being destroyed as a result of these attributes—human attributes that have been around since Genesis, well before the development of capitalism.

Most agree that God requires we be good stewards of the resources put under our control, which is why we need to consider how best to generate prosperity. This, too, is illustrated in parable after parable by Jesus. However, the remaining question for the faithful steward of resources is what to do next, after wealth has been created.

Now the billionaire that I am referring to in the earlier paragraph is, by reputation, an extremely generous man. Also, he can rightly argue that by faithfully growing his fortune, he can do more good with the money now than had he given it away earlier. And he is right. However, as Alcorn reminds us, we need to consider God's designs for the resources that He puts under our control. What if God had purposed that this wealth should have been deployed earlier, helping the millions of people that have died from disease or malnourishment in the years during which it had been accumulated? Although we cannot definitively know God's designs, we do know that God holds us accountable for helping others whose material blessings may not be the same as ours. He expects us to care for this world, and to care for one another, and His timing is not the same as ours. All of these principles together help to create a sense of urgency about giving that may be inconsistent with our natural impulses.

Does anyone really need a billion dollars? The Bible tells us that we are blessed to be a blessing. Hoarding the abundance God bestows on us seems inconsistent with that notion, so it seems inconsistent with abiding faith. We don't need to hoard because we can rely on God. But, this is not just an issue for billionaires. This is an issue for just about all of us in the DEVELOPED world. We have more than enough, yet there are many, many people on the earth who live at or below subsistence levels.

In his book, Alcorn indicates that obstacles to giving include "unbelief, insecurity, pride, idolatry, desire for power and control" and, most importantly, "the illusion that the earth is our home." He offers plenty of scriptural references, primarily New Testament references, which support his argument that, considering our ultimate destination, we should be laying up treasures in heaven, not on earth, since that is where we are meant to be. He points out that "We'll each part with our money. The only question is when. We have no choice but to part with it later (when we die). But we do have a choice (about) whether to part with it now. We can keep earthly treasures for a moment, and we may enjoy some temporary enjoyment from them. But if we give them away, we'll enjoy eternal treasures that will never be taken from us."

I am not going to try to summarize Alcorn's entire book. You can read it in an evening. But, I am asking you to please do read it, as it may change your life. I was so impressed by it that not only did it change my pattern and approach to charitable giving, but I also started handing out copies of the book to others. Almost every person found its message to be transformational. You may do the same. If you do, you will find yourself donating more, and donating more consistently. You will become more conscious of deploying God's assets to God's causes and, as a result, more conscious of God. It will draw you closer to God in a way that writing checks at tax time never could.

Only you can determine what level of giving makes sense for you. I know from my own personal experience that it is more than I would have guessed—and that it is very freeing to live less materially. As the present financial crisis indicates, materialism isn't all that it is cracked up to be. Over time, we become more certain of this, and the percentage of our income that we are willing to give away starts to grow.

The traditional definition of a tithe is ten percent of one's income. I know people who have given much more than that percentage, because they are extraordinarily generous and their resources permit a higher level of giving. The challenge is to get started. Once we do that, things start to develop a momentum of their own; but the key, if we desire personal transformation and deeper faith, is to start now.

Tithing seems to fall under the larger role of stewardship, one of the primary roles given to man at the time of creation. The Bible tells us that God entrusted man with the stewardship of the entire earth. From a business perspective, authority and responsibility need to go hand in hand. If our authority extends to the entire world, then our responsibility does as well. The Bible also tells us that in establishing the covenant with Abraham, the covenant by which He was going to bless "all people," God had some conditions for the people He blesses. In relaying those conditions, one of the things that God says is "And from each man, too, I will demand an accounting from the life of his fellow man" (Genesis 9:5). Regardless of the original context, this verse suggests that we truly are our brother's keeper. From a global perspective, we have a lot of work to do.

It makes sense to approach any big task by breaking it down into smaller tasks. In the area of charitable giving, if we are concerned about the stewardship of the resources we donate, we can use the internet and other means to research how well charities steward the resources that they are given. One example of such a resource is Charity Navigator®.[19] Although this resource may not measure the effectiveness of a charity in meeting its stated goals, it does provide some perspective on whether those goals are being met efficiently, which is one aspect of proper stewardship.

Another thing that we can do is to establish a charitable-giving account with just about any of the major fund houses. There are many advantages to establishing an account like this, including: it makes it easy for us to contribute our desired percentage of income immediately (and, in my case, without excuses); it provides professional management of the funds until they are ultimately disbursed, it offers excellent and simplified accounting for tax purposes, and it provides additional online resources to assist us in evaluating the charities that we fund.

As a last word on the subject of tithing, consider how often the Bible refers to fearing God. In the past, this concept always seemed alien to me; there is no need to fear a loving God. But I have come to wonder whether this is one of the areas of human life that the Biblical writers were thinking about when they wrote. Would a Holy God approve of how we have managed the blessings He has bestowed upon us? Are we cheerfully extending those blessings to others, or are we keeping them for ourselves and our loved ones? What are God's intentions? I worry that I have too much, and that I have shared too little, and that in doing so I have fallen FAR SHORT of God's high expectations. But, being pragmatic, I also fear that the economy and markets are bad, and that I may outlive "my" money.

Such worries are inconsistent with abiding faith. For many of us, most especially those who have enjoyed some measure of material success, this is a perfect area to put our faith to the test, to pray for strength, to thank God for His forgiveness and to do more to respond to the will of God. As we do so, our faith grows.

DISCUSSION/STUDY QUESTIONS FOR CHAPTER SEVEN

1. Some Christians believe that the unequal distribution of wealth of this world is a symptom of the fall of man. Others believe that God wants to prosper us in every way and that material abundance is part of God's blessing. Both views are supported by the Bible. How do you reconcile the two perspectives?

2. What does the Bible say about tithing? What did Jesus have to say on the topic? Does that fact that government may coerce giving through taxation and income redistribution have any bearing on God's desire for us to extend His blessings to others by giving generously? Does the amount that you pay in taxes affect your approach to charitable giving?

3. Jesus warns that we may never know when our time on earth may be up and we will be called to account for how we lived. What does that imply in terms of the sense of urgency we should have with respect to charitable intentions? Does having a will that distributes our money and property after we are gone let us off the hook from following Jesus in this particular area of our lives while we're alive?

CHAPTER EIGHT

BE STILL

BE STILL AND KNOW THAT I AM GOD; I WILL BE EXALTED AMONG THE NATIONS, I WILL BE EXALTED IN THE EARTH.
(PSALMS 46:10)

Many of us live lives that can only be characterized as frenzied. We work most of the day; we hustle the kids around to their after-school activities, and we collapse in front of the television at the end of the day. We get too little sleep, and then we start all over again the next day. On the weekends, we cram our schedules so that we can have quality "family time." Then many of us spend an hour or so at church trying to attune ourselves to God.

Although we may "feel better" after spending time at church, if we are not taking what we learn into the rest of the week, the odds of this hour being truly effective in deepening our faith, or changing our lives, may be low. In fact, for many of us, the good feeling that we may have after an hour at church is lost before we leave the church parking lot, perhaps because that self-centered so-and-so cut us off on the way out, or because we know that we need to run to the grocery store after church and the kids despise going to the grocery store.

Thankfully, God is so aware of our propensity for losing touch with Him, and the consequences of our losing touch, that

He provided us the Sabbath rest. He literally "set in stone" the idea that we need to take a day away from our busy lives every week to be with Him. He set apart a whole day, not an hour, because he knew how restorative that day could be for us, if we truly observed it. Unfortunately, many of us have convinced ourselves that we don't have time to do this. The reality, though, is that we don't have time not to do it.

Faith aside, there are practical reasons for us to take time out of our busy lives, to empty our minds of our day to day distractions and just "be." People of just about every culture have been doing this for years, some more skillfully than others, and research shows that the centeredness that follows the practice can benefit just about every aspect of our lives, at home, at work, and at play.

For example, experts in creativity inform us that most creative breakthroughs occur not immediately after the period of hard work to gather and distill all the facts around a situation, but after an "incubation" period during which we set our project aside and let those thoughts simmer. People who coach athletes talk about the benefits of mental training, time spent not actually doing what they do for a living, but visualizing it, most especially for peak athletic performers.

Although we don't live it, most of us probably intuitively accept the idea of the benefits of meditative practice. We can easily conjure in our heads the notion of the composed Zen master, totally content and centered while sitting still in meditation. We are familiar with the concept of "no mind" and the benefits of tuning into our more enlightened selves, but we still don't do it. The pressures not to do it are relentless, both at home and at work. Unfortunately, the technological advances of the last couple of decades have made the problem worse, because now we can carry our work with us everywhere.

Nearly twenty years ago, my father decided to retire. My immediate reaction was to start thinking of things for him to do—for example, start a company designed to capitalize on the demographics of people retiring, or use his experiences to write a book that considered the behavioral and psychological aspects of retirement and that addressed financial security and the need to stay productive. When I offered these ideas to him, I remember my father remarking, positively, that I had a restive mind. At the time, I really liked this characterization of myself.

What I have come to believe, though, is that my mind has always been a bit too restive and not enough at rest. I was so focused on doing "things," that I rarely took the time just to "be." And, while there were discernible, short-term, material benefits to having done this, it no doubt contributed to the creeping near-agnosticism I described earlier, the consequences of which could be eternal.

Almost invariably, one aspect of being hard-working and productive is a certain level of material success, which reinforces the desire to work hard and to be productive. Before too long, we start to look at almost anything that gets in the way of getting things done as an impediment to be removed, and we start to define ourselves in terms of our work and accomplishments. This insidious movement from who we are to what we do is nothing less than a tragedy.

The Bible tells us that we are children of God, made in the image of God. Imagine that, we are children of God made in the image of God! Nothing that we can do to define ourselves can be bigger or better than that. If we start with this identity and cultivate it, we can be so much more than if we start with any other, by definition, more limiting concept of ourselves. But in order to cultivate this identity, we need to know God well enough to identify with Him, hence the need to "be still."

Unfortunately, many of us have been "not still" for so long, that we have forgotten the art of being still. It is just too easy to distract ourselves by doing things. Consider what happens when we have nothing to do. Do we sit there and say, "Ah, finally, a moment to just sit and be still, to quiet my mind and rest in God's presence"? For most of us, the answer to this is probably not. More likely, we start doing something, or reading something, or revising our to-do lists, or turning on the television or surfing the internet, or otherwise busying ourselves with the few spare minutes we have before our next scheduled commitment.

So, how can people who are not practiced in being still begin the practice? One answer to this is "Do something," since that is what we're best at, anyway. But we need to make that something an activity that naturally leads toward stillness.

Take a walk along the beach, but leave your iPod and the family dog at home when you do. Smell the air; listen to the waves and perhaps the sounds of the sea gulls; feel the warmth of the sun on your face and the cool of the water on your feet; search for sea glass. Before too long, the rhythms of the place will transport you miles from the typical bustle of your life, and you will be still. Speaking personally, I have experienced God at the shoreline countless times.

Take a walk in the nearest forest preserve. Listen to the rustling of the leaves, the snow beneath your feet or the shushing of squirrels about the forest floor. Feel the breeze on your face and watch the leaves get caught up in it; spinning, twisting, and circling, before they softly land. Your worldly concerns will diminish, and you will sense the presence of God. Acknowledge that presence and savor the feeling of it. Be still.

Get up half an hour early and write in your journal. Lay your concerns before God and simply let them be. Listen quietly and see whether you notice your sub-conscious self working out solutions to your problems or whether you notice that those problems just don't seem as big anymore, now that you have laid your cares before the Lord. Consider how blessed your life is, even during the most troublesome times. Be still.

Pull out your Bible, but before you open it, sit silently and ask God to speak to you as you read it. Take a long pause just to be still.

Such activities help us to savor the quiet moments of our lives and to know how to use such moments when they come to us. We become less inclined to turn on the television and more inclined to savor the silence that such moments encourage and to feel the presence of God. We begin to experience the abundance of the natural world around us that we once ignored because we were "too busy," and we come to know that God IS. This is the great treasure to be found in stillness.

Most of us are aware of the physiological benefits of meditation, but there is no question that the effects of being still go far beyond such benefits. My guess is that it is because we are surrendering to God. In being still, we're not worrying about what happened yesterday or earlier today, and we're not working out in our heads what we should be doing tomorrow. Instead, we are quieting ourselves, emptying our minds, and making space for God to enter into our hearts. It seems that when we create those conditions, God is happy to fill the space that we have created for Him.

Nothing can take the place of a personal encounter with God. Nobody can tell you what it feels like, and it may not feel the same for you, in any case, even if they could. What you can be sure of is that once you have been touched by God in this way you will never, ever doubt again His existence or His involvement in our lives. So, begin a regular practice of making some space in your life, apart from the usual bustle and prattle of your typical day; learn to empty your mind of your cares and concerns; learn to listen and to be still, and your faith will begin to grow.

DISCUSSION/STUDY QUESTIONS FOR CHAPTER EIGHT

1. When was the last time that you observed a Sabbath day – an entire day when you did no work and used that day with the intention of getting closer to God?

2. Do you feel centered? What activities do you enjoy that promote that condition for you? Do you make a regular practice of engaging in those activities? What aspects of your life would benefit from the centeredness that comes from stillness?

3. Do you have a voice inside your head, practically audible, that evaluates and interprets almost everything that you see, do, hear or say? Does that voice at times cause you unnecessary consternation? How might deeper faith help to quiet that voice and to allow you to more fully experience your life without the constant din of evaluation and interpretation?

4. Have you ever had a strong sense of God's presence? What were you doing at the time? What did it feel like? Why do you think that you had that feeling and how can you make time to experience it again?

CHAPTER NINE

BECOME PART OF A CHURCH

AND YOU ARE AMONG THOSE CALLED TO BELONG TO JESUS CHRIST.
(ROMANS 1:6)

As I have mentioned before, I was a self-help junkie who had always believed pretty strongly in self-determinism. I also happen to be naturally introverted, so my inclination often has been to do things on my own. And if I have any success in the publishing process, there is a pretty good chance that you picked up this book in the "self-help" section of the book store, because I truly believe that seeking God is an individual pursuit to which we need to dedicate ourselves in order to succeed. Accordingly, this book is, in a sense, a self-help manual for faith, and you may have bought it because you like the idea of pursuing this endeavor on your own.

Unfortunately, the time has come to let you down by saying I don't believe you can do this entirely on your own. There is no doubt that we can get a long way on our own, but at some point it helps to become part of the church and to actively participate in it. Sorry, but that just seems to be the way it is. In fact, if you have been reading the Bible, you no doubt are well past that part of Scripture where God reflects on all of His creation and says that it is "good," but He observes that man alone is "not good" (Genesis 2:18). This and other passages in the Bible make clear that God intends for us to be part of a community of believers.

Logically, if we're listening for God, we may as well go where people are likely to talk about Him. Church is one such place. Also, it seems that Jesus expected that we should worship communally, with the promised benefit that "where two or three come together, there I am with them" (Matthew 18:20). So, it seems that worshipping God is, by its nature, a team sport, at least some of the time.

Our worship and our faith can be greatly enhanced by joining a church. The use of music and song deepens our spiritual experience. For example, I am not one for rote memorization, but I have, without even trying, memorized a lot of Scripture through song. I would not have done this on my own. Similarly, our church has facilitated the formation of Bible study groups. To be honest, I doubt that I would have engaged in group Bible study without this encouragement from the church. Being part of a church allows us to place our natural proclivities aside in favor of actively participating in our chosen spiritual community. This participation is extremely important and very enabling. Jesus was on a mission to transform the world and He wants us, the church, to be part of that mission.

At the risk of being branded a heretic, though, I'll offer that I believe that if you are not Christian, and you wish to deepen your faith, then start with a place that suits your own culture and religious traditions, whether that is a temple, a mosque or some other location. My guess is that God will get through to you there.

My basis for believing this is the Bible. When God made the covenant with Abraham, he said "I will bless you...AND ALL PEOPLES ON EARTH WILL BE BLESSED THROUGH YOU" (Genesis 12:2-3). In Acts

10:34, we read that "God does not show favoritism, but ACCEPTS MEN FROM EVERY NATION who fear him and do what is right." In Revelation 5:9-10, God promises that heaven will be filled with the redeemed from "EVERY TRIBE AND LANGUAGE, PEOPLE AND NATION."

Although I am aware that Jesus stated "I am the way and the truth and the life. No one comes to the Father except through me" (John 14:6), I also know that the Bible illustrates that God appears to men in many forms. In fact, the risen Christ appeared to His disciples in a form that they did not immediately recognize[20], and that same Jesus also promised "knock and the door will be opened...He who seeks finds" (Matthew 7:7-8). Surely a well-intentioned pursuit of God through one's own traditions is a form of "asking, seeking, and knocking."[21] Finally, Jesus, when he walked on earth, by definition did not encounter any Christians until after he converted them to faith in Him. Why would we believe that He would not be willing to continue to do this today?

Since Jesus was welcoming of both sinners and saints, it follows that one of the more important aspects of any institution we attend should be that it is welcoming. That is the very nature of community. If a church is not welcoming, it is not modeling Jesus very well. This does not imply that the church should accord us full membership without requiring us to accept its doctrines. A church has to stand for something, and it is reasonable for the church to call for its members to stand for those same things. As we read in Isaiah, "If you do not stand firm in your faith, you will not stand at all" (Isaiah 7:9). Importantly, this requires us to know exactly what it is that our church believes and to consider whether we are willing to embrace those same things.

The New Testament describes the church as the body of Christ, with Christ at the head. Although one would think that this would imply some unanimity of thought, the body is composed of people—and people don't always agree on things. Disagreement among Christians started very in the early the history of the Christian church, very shortly after the time of Christ, as evidenced by the many letters of Paul. However, one thing that Christian churches seem to agree on is the core beliefs expressed in the Apostles' Creed, which expresses believers' faith in the triune God, Jesus Christ's virgin birth, his crucifixion, death and resurrection, the forgiveness of sins, our own future resurrection, and life everlasting. It seems that the reason people of faith can agree on the Creed is that it is supportable by the Bible. By implication, any church that purports to be Christian and professes a different basis of faith should be viewed very suspiciously.

One of the things that Christian churches seem to disagree on is the status of Mary, the mother of Jesus. Mary is accorded very high status in the Catholic Church. In fact, in the church of my youth, nearly every mass included a recitation of the "Hail Mary," which affirms her as the "mother of God" and invokes her as an intercessor, asking that she "pray for us sinners." In contrast, some non-Catholic Christian churches hardly seem to acknowledge Mary at all. The reasons for this seem to be a concern that too much focus on Mary might cause people to equate her with Jesus; the fact that there isn't really much said about Mary in the Bible; the belief that God could have selected

83

anyone to bear Jesus; and reservations about intercessory prayer.

I currently belong to a non-denominational Christian church, and I have to admit that Mary seems conspicuous by her absence. In stark contrast to the church of my childhood years, I cannot recall a single mention of Mary in my current church at any time during the several years I have attended it. For reasons I will articulate later, I decided to get over my reservations about the apparent relegation of Mary to seemingly second-class citizen status, because of everything that is so very good about the church. Having said this, I believe it is possible to honor Mary, who was chosen by God to bear her Son—and who evidenced extraordinary faith in agreeing to do so—without stepping over the bounds of suggesting equivalence with Jesus. It seems to me that the church is mistaken in not considering her more closely.

For those of you interested in the topic, *Mary for Evangelicals* by Tim Perry,[22] does an excellent job of surveying the history of Mary in various Christian traditions. It is an excellent resource for those wanting to know more about Mary and the differing perceptions of her.

Now I went off on this little diatribe for one reason and one reason only: to point out that belonging to a church and accepting its core beliefs is not the same as agreeing with everything it says, doesn't say, does or doesn't do. My own, admittedly somewhat limited view of this is that there is more alike about the various Christian traditions than different. At least they all seem to agree on the most important matter of faith in Jesus Christ. I sometimes don't understand why so much emphasis is placed on the differences. However, I recognize that some differences do matter, because they are fundamental to the faith as expressed by the church, so it is very important for us to be vigilant in understanding them. When in doubt, though, it seems that a good starting point for talking with other earnestly-faithful people can be found in Romans 15:7 which says "Accept one another, then, just as Christ accepted you, in order to bring praise to God."

Beyond adherence to the core doctrines of the Apostles' Creed, a church should offer leaders who understand and can teach us about the Bible. The Bible is the Word of God, and the more we know about it, the more we will be able to understand it. The more we understand it, the closer our relationships with God will be, and the more our faith will grow as a result. However, we need to be very cautious about those who try to augment the Bible or to take away from what it says. The Bible warns against this practice.[23] Although we want the leaders of the church to be schooled enough in the Bible to give us historical context, we should be very wary when they deviate from what the Bible actually says.

One of the main aspects of a church is vital, communal worship of God. If yours is missing that, then you're missing out on a lot. If you attend church and the service has become routine for you, and you are convinced that it is not because of you, then you may need to help change your church or to find another church. While it may be better to "go through the motions" than to not attend at all, going through the motions is a poor substitute for experiencing God while joyously worshipping with fellow Christians. The experience should energize us for the week, when we're back in a world that often doesn't naturally offer the same opportunity.

Finally, it helps to be aware that some churches do a very good job of engaging their parishioners beyond the church walls. They are very effective at setting up small groups, providing spiritual resources, organizing community involvement and supporting and organizing mission trips. If your church is not good at these things, perhaps you can help. These types of genuine Christian outreach are both energizing and contagious, and they greatly influenced our decision to join our current church.

It is important that we don't short-change our church life by giving it just one hour a week and that we don't try to "do" our spiritual life all alone. Rather, by becoming part of the church, we grab hold of Jesus' promise that "when two or three of you are gathered, I will be with you." Our faith is strengthened through our relationship with other believers.

DISCUSSION/STUDY QUESTIONS FOR CHAPTER NINE

1. When discussing this chapter with the senior pastor of my church, he reminded me of the story of the return of the prodigal son. Read Luke 15:11-32 with some emphasis on the behavior of the brother of the returning son. How might our own "righteous indignity" keep others from joining, or returning to, the church?

2. It has been said that you cannot join the church of your dreams, you have to make it. What areas of your church do you feel need improvement? How can you help?

3. Some people, both Christians and, especially, non-Christians, are troubled by John 14:6. How do we reconcile this verse with God's expressed intention to bless all people? What is the role of Christian believers in God's plan? What is your role?

4. I once read that we cannot bring people to Jesus, but we can bring Jesus to people. Can you think of three tangible ways to extend the love of God to another person?

CHAPTER TEN

GROW IN GOD'S GRACE

WE BELIEVE THAT IT IS THROUGH THE GRACE OF OUR LORD JESUS THAT WE ARE SAVED. (ACTS 15:11)

Like "bang," "buzz," or "clang," "grace" sounds something like what it is: a cleansing, sanctifying gift from God by which He repairs the broken relationship between God and man. Most Christian denominations seem to agree that God's grace is at the center of His relationship with mankind, because without God's grace we would be forever separated from God due to our sinful nature.

It seems the "problem" that causes the need for grace is found in the very nature of God, as articulated by God Himself to Moses, in Exodus, chapter 34: "Yet he does not leave the guilty unpunished; he punishes the children and their children for the sins of the fathers to the third and fourth generation" (Exodus 34:7). A holy God cannot tolerate sin, so sin causes separation from God, and ultimately death. Thankfully, that same section of Scripture tells us that God's name also includes, "The LORD, the compassionate and gracious God, slow to anger, abounding in love and faithfulness, maintaining love to thousands and forgiving wickedness, rebellion and sin" (Exodus 34:6-7). In other words, also inherent to God's nature are mercy and grace. These attributes of God and our inherent imperfection require some resolution, which is why Jesus Christ was born, suffered, died and rose from the dead, so that our sins could be forgiven and our relationship with God restored. God's grace is our salvation and our source of new life, through the death and resurrection of Jesus Christ.

Although this seems simple enough, this is an area that seems to have caused heated debate among Christian churches throughout time. The devil is in the details, I guess.

What is the role of human will if God's will is to extend us grace? Don't we still have some accountability? If our actions don't evidence the fact that we have been saved, how can we tell if God's grace was ever received? Can we fall out of grace? If we do fall from grace, what, if anything, can we do about that? What is the role of the church in all of this? Since we are born sinners and destined to continue sinning, is the situation basically hopeless?

There are Christians who believe God has pre-ordained those who will receive grace. This would be very bad news indeed for those whom God has not so favored. To me, this seems a bit inconsistent with a loving God and the many references to God's desire to bless all people. Also, it is difficult for me to understand why a Christian would hold this view. What is the purpose of the life, suffering, and death of Jesus, if our fate is pre-ordained by God? God's preordination would imply that there was nothing at all left to do, so why would He bother to send His Son?

Despite all the controversy around the idea of grace, Scripture makes clear—and most denominations seem to agree—that there is nothing we can do to earn the gift of grace offered by God. We simply don't deserve it. However, Scripture also says that there is something that we must do in order to receive it: We must repent from our sins and put our faith in Jesus Christ. That is why this book is about faith. Faith is important because it is through faith that we are saved—"righteousness from God comes through faith in Jesus Christ" (Romans 3:22). So, as someone once put it, grace is God's part and faith is man's responsibility.

Terrific. Now we have a nice neat and tidy package: we put our faith in Jesus and, since there's nothing else that we can do to merit God's grace anyway, there's nothing else that we must do, so we can go on living our lives the way we'd like and rest assured that our faith will get us into heaven. How freeing this gospel thing is!

Not exactly. In preparing to write this chapter, knowing that the subject of grace was one of the major issues among the various Christian denominations, I did a little reading. I found that the belief articulated in the prior paragraph is called "antinomianism." The Merriam-Webster online dictionary[24] tells us that an antinomian is: 1) one who holds that under the gospel dispensation of grace the moral law is of no use or obligation because faith alone is necessary to salvation 2) one who rejects a socially established morality. Evidently, the antinomians reared their heads pretty early in the history of Christianity, because Paul found it necessary to put the idea to rest in one of his letters, rhetorically asking, "Shall we go on sinning so that grace may increase?"(Romans 6:1) Paul immediately answers this question, saying: "By no means! We died to sin; how can we live it any longer" (Romans 6:2). So, Paul established that we have a responsibility to live differently once grace has been received.

But antinomianism seems pretty extreme, and it is not the only source of vexation among various branches of Christianity. I brought it up on the unlikely chance that someone actually nodded his or her head when I wrote the penultimate paragraph above. All of the other issues and concerns at center of the controversy are embodied in the questions listed earlier: *What is the role of human will if God's will is to extend us grace? Don't we still have some accountability? If our actions don't evidence the fact that we have been saved, how can we tell if God's grace was ever received? Can we fall out of grace? If we do, what, if anything, can we do about that? What is the role of the church in all of this? Since we are born sinners and destined to continue sinning, is the situation basically hopeless?* Perhaps, like some early Christians suggested, we should postpone our baptisms until we're about to die, since there is no chance to stop sinning before that time!

Without trying to reconcile all of the differences of the various denominations of Christian churches (which gives rise to different doctrines, sacraments and their meanings, governance structures, etcetera), it seems there are a few things we all can agree on. Let's start with those things.

First, when we are offered a wonderful gift—particularly a gift that we could never afford—by all means we should take it. The path provided in the Bible is to recognize that we are sinners and to place our faith in the fact that Jesus has TAKEN AWAY our sins through His life, death and resurrection. Although we will continue sinning, those sins have already been atoned for, once and for all, after we repent from our sins, put our faith in Jesus and, as a result, receive God's grace. Psalm 51: 1-6, as written in *The Message* translation, provides a terrific starting point for initiating our relationship with Jesus: "Generous in love—God, give grace! Huge in mercy—wipe out my bad record. Scrub away my guilt; soak out my sins in your laundry. I know how bad I've been; my sins are staring me down. You're the One I've violated, and you've seen it all, seen the full extent of my evil. You have all the facts before you; whatever you decide about me is fair. I've been out of step with you for a long time, in the wrong since before I was born. What you're after is truth from the inside out. Enter me, then; conceive a new, true life."[25] Jesus echoes the last sentence of this Old Testament psalm when He tells us that "no one can see the kingdom of God unless he is born again" (John 3:3).

Looking at the origins of the word, true repentance implies some regret for our sins and a change of heart and mind in seeking God's forgiveness for them. It seems that Jesus' suggestion of the need to be born again includes the notion that we really need to start over and that it may not be easy. Once we have truly received Jesus, we simply cannot remain the person who we brought to Him; once we have truly received Him, we have become, and we need to continue to become, a new person.

Second, when we are offered an extraordinary gift, we probably all agree that we should fully appreciate the gift. We can begin by being aware of its attributes. Grace "teaches us to say 'No' to ungodliness and worldly passions, and to live self-controlled, upright, and godly lives in this present age" (Titus 2:12). The Bible tells us that God's grace can "scrub away my guilt"[26] (Psalms 51:2), and that because of His grace He "makes everything come out right...He doesn't treat us as our sins deserve, nor pay us back in full for our wrong" (Psalms 103: 6,10).

Then, we can use the gift. The Bible does seem to warn that grace can be received in vain[27] and urges us to grow in grace and in our faith, making "every effort to add to your faith goodness; and to goodness, knowledge; and to knowledge, self-control; and to self-control, perseverance; and to perseverance, godliness; and to godliness, brotherly kindness; and to brotherly kindness, love" (2 Peter 1:5-7), with the goal of remaining effective and productive in our "knowledge of our Lord Jesus Christ" (2 Peter 1:8). Although this is the goal, history shows that we will not succeed. Still, the Bible exhorts us to try.

Unfortunately, although this is an area of interpretation among the faithful, there does seem to be the risk of "use it or lose it," or that we can fall from grace, which the Bible says is evidenced by our continuing to sin.[28] And the Bible suggests that the consequences of doing so may be worse than never having received grace at all.[29] Yet we all do continue to sin, so does that imply that God's grace is not effective?

As the study portion of my Bible says, "God sees our struggle all too well. He does not expect new Christians to mature and bear fruit overnight. But (the biblical author of) John emphasizes increasing conformity of a person's will to the will of God."[30] This suggests that we should be concerned if we do not genuinely feel a transformation occurring within us, or if we have no desire to change at all, because it could evidence that we have not actually been saved. The Bible warns that, "If the wicked are shown grace, they don't seem to get it. In the land of right living, they persist in wrong living, blind to the splendor of GOD" (Isaiah 26:10).[31]

Fourth, when given an extraordinary gift, we can share it with others. That is very much part of what this book is about for me. St. Paul's transformation was so complete that he changed from a persecutor of Christians to the leading preacher of the gospel. The gospel that he preached, given to us, is that "by the gift of God's grace...through faith in Christ Jesus, we may approach God in freedom and confidence" (Ephesians 3:7, 12).

Finally, we can do our best to return the love of the giver. Jesus made this simple for us, telling us that we show our love for Him by obeying his commands (John 14:21). As if that were not simple enough, Jesus further simplified our task by telling us the two most important commandments: "Love the Lord your God with all your heart, your mind, and your soul...and love your neighbor as yourself" (Mark 12:29).

Clearly, our faith can be a living faith, expressed by a change in our self-centered nature toward one that is more focused on others. Peterson's translation of 1 Corinthians 10:23-24 summarizes the matter of the receipt of God's grace and its implications for our actions very well: "Looking at it one way, you could say, 'Anything goes. Because of God's immense generosity and grace, we don't have to dissect and scrutinize every action to see if it will pass muster.' But the point is not to just get by. We want to live well, but our foremost efforts should be to help *others* live well."

DISCUSSION/STUDY QUESTIONS FOR CHAPTER TEN

1. God could have created perfect human beings. Why did He create us the way He did, knowing that we would get off track?

2. What does it mean to say that our sins have been taken away, when we know that we will continue to sin? How might the notion that nothing that we can do can again separate us from God be perverted to excuse or justify sinful behavior?

3. If we continue to sin, does that evidence that we have not received God's grace or that God's grace is somehow insufficient? Can you point to two or three scripture versus that support your point of view? What distinguishes the recipient of grace from the one who has not received it?

4. Jesus often rebukes the Pharisees, who at times seem to be making a sincere effort to live cleaner lives. What was missing from the practice of their faith? How can we be certain that we are sincere in our faith?

CHAPTER ELEVEN

SURRENDER TO GOD'S WILL

YOU NEED TO PERSEVERE, SO THAT WHEN YOU HAVE DONE THE WILL OF GOD, YOU WILL RECEIVE WHAT HE PROMISED.
(HEBREWS 10:36)

As implied by the last chapter, and stated very directly throughout the Bible, God's promises to us are conditional; the condition that we must meet is that we do what He says. This requires two things from us. First, we must submit to God's sovereignty, rather than our own will. Second, we need to ascertain what it is that He wants us to do. Neither may prove easy.

Most of us have struggled with the idea of God's sovereignty on one level or another. Submission does not come easily to those of us who have a strong desire to be self-determined. Alternatively, we may look at the world around us and presume that God is not active in our world, because of what we see. Surveying the landscape, we may struggle with the very existence and/or the nature of God, losing touch with our belief and the purpose of our lives.

Dysteleology is the philosophical view that our existence has no final cause. People who adhere to this point of view believe that there either is no God behind the universe, because the world is full of pain and evil; or that God is malevolent, because he permits pain and evil; or, perhaps He is not sovereign, because He would not permit evil if it were in His control.

People who see the world this way see natural disasters such as hurricanes, droughts or typhoons, or man-made tragedies, such as war, genocide, or the attacks of September 11, 2001, as evidence of the proposition that God does not exist or, if He does, that He is not what we think He is...or should be. Some people abandon their faith after considering such things. In their minds, God and these things cannot co-exist. Since it is clear that bad things can happen and evil does exist, then perhaps God does not. In that case, perhaps the best we can hope for is that we all, in following our own designs, treat each other civilly.

In contrast, the faithful can take a "glass half-full" view of the world. Sure, there are natural disasters that test our faith and indeed Satan is at work on this planet, but we can trust in God, because He is at work, too. Yes, there are wars, and famine and horrible attacks like those on the Twin Towers on September 11th, but God can be found in all of these circumstances. God is present in the soldier who saves his fallen comrade, the missionary bringing food to impoverished areas where most people would fear to tread, and in the firemen and the emergency workers who went into those towers when everyone else was trying to get out. Where the good is present in such terrible circumstances is where God can be found.

Believers accept that God has a plan for us. We don't always know what the plan is, and that can be very frustrating at times, but we know He has a plan. So, we place our faith in God; we look for the good while slogging through the bad, knowing that God is at work, perhaps molding our character for some other endeavor. Although we accept God's sovereignty, and we believe that some good will come out of even seemingly terrible circumstances, we may still find ourselves frustrated. We wonder why God doesn't give us clearer signals about our role in the world or in any particular circumstance. How can we follow God if we don't know what He wants us to do? At such times, we might conclude that all we can do is look for the good, put our shoulders to the wheel, and press on.

However, there can be pitfalls in looking for the good. The problem with seeking "the good" in any particular situation is that what is good for one person may not be good for another. We can be remarkably adroit at misleading other people, and ourselves, if we become too hazy in our focus on what is truly good. We might find ourselves bending the truth or leaving out little bits of it, because we think that some greater good needs to be served. What's a little lie or embellishment if it gets the right result? Surely, God would want the greater good to be served, right?

Scripture is one place to look for the answer to such questions. Based upon Jesus' experience on earth, it is clear that He took the side of telling the truth, even though it led to His own suffering and death on the cross. Jesus had the opportunity to get Himself off the hook by denying His true identity. He could have convinced himself that there was a greater good in His extending His stay here on earth. Clearly, He was anguished by where God the Father was leading Him; He prayed that there might be some other answer. But that was not the will of the Father, so Jesus did as the Father willed. Following Jesus, which requires following His example, is not always easy.

As this example illustrates, sometimes we are faced with painful choices, where doing the right thing is certain to result in a difficult time for us. At such times, we have to resist the urge to put God's intentions into a neat little box that just happens to align with our view of the circumstances—our hoped-for outcome that also happens to be easy to do.

It isn't always easy to do what is right. We should be skeptical if it always seems to work out that way for us. God's path may be the difficult one.

Perhaps we are willing to serve, even if it may imply some trials, but we sincerely do not know what God wishes. What do we do then? First, we should take heart. The very fact that we desire to know His will and that we stand ready to submit to it shows that God is at work in our lives. Still, we need to go about the work of discerning God's intentions.

In the book *Experiencing God*[32] by Henry Blackaby and Claude King, the authors offer the following advice for discerning God's will in such situations: pray, watch carefully what happens after you pray, make connections between your prayers and what happens next, ask probing questions of the people you encounter, listen carefully to what they tell you and then "Be ready to make whatever adjustments are required in order to join God in what He is doing." Importantly, THE KEY IS NOT TO SEEK GOD'S BLESSINGS, BUT TO LET GOD WORK THROUGH YOU. "When you begin to see God moving, adjust your life and respond."

The book goes on to address confusing or difficult circumstances, noting that "You can't know the truth of your circumstances until you have heard from God." The authors caution, "Never, ever determine the truth of a situation by looking (only) at the circumstances." They observe that often our choices are not between two things, one obviously good or the other obviously bad. Sometimes our choices are between what is good versus what is best. "The place to start is to say WITH ALL OF YOUR HEART (emphasis added) Lord, whatever I know to be your will, I will do. Regardless of the cost and regardless of the adjustment, I will follow." They urge that we commit to do this BEFORE we seek God's will, lest we run the risk of seeking God's will "as long as it does not conflict with (our own)."

"Following God will require faith and action. Without faith you will not be able to please God. When you act in faith, God is pleased." The authors warn that joining God may require some substantial adjustments, noting that we cannot stay where we are and join God at the same time. "Part of knowing and doing the will of God (is)...coming to total dependence on God," which requires complete trust in God. Our "obedience is the moment of truth."

Certainly, we have all read about lives transformed by obedience to God. Deep in our souls we all desire to know God's will in a way that encourages us to such obedience. But God works across eternity. His will may be very difficult to discern, given our much more limited view. In such circumstances, it helps to focus on what is more immediate and in our control, to be mindful and honest with ourselves about our motives, and to recognize that the bulk of our lives are spent doing small things, rather than making momentous decisions. By paying attention to the present moment, really paying attention, we can, in each moment, choose the way that leads away from or toward surrendering our lives to God, honoring Him by choosing the latter course.

This simplifies things. We can sit and worry about doing God's will, or we can exercise our creative talents in the present moment to honor God. The longer we sit and worry, the longer we may be unhappy or unsatisfied, because the Bible tells us that God has specific intentions for us and part of our life's journey is fulfilling that purpose: "For we are God's workmanship, created in Christ Jesus to do good works, which God has prepared in advance for us to do" (Ephesians 2:10).

In other words, Scripture tells us that we have a calling, and that part of our life's journey and spiritual development is fulfilling that calling. An excellent book on this topic is Gregg LeVoy's *Callings: Finding and Following an Authentic Life*.[33] The title alone tells you much. This book is a gem for seekers.

LeVoy offers that "generally, people will not pursue their callings until the fear of doing so is finally exceeded by the pain of not doing so." What causes us to wait so long? Perhaps what gets in our way is our self-will. LeVoy tells us that "we have to be willing to surrender;" importantly, "this surrender is about liberation, not defeat." It is about "giving up the transitory for the sake of the transcendent."

LeVoy cautions that resistance is a natural response to a calling. We have trouble leaving behind who we are so that we can move forward toward what we are to become. This is why we need things like "money in the bank, a plan to fall back on, a support group, and people who believe in us" if we are to pursue our callings. The purpose of these safety nets is not to plan to fail, but to provide the proper foundation for moving forward, which we may have to do in small steps, the critical advantage of which is the information that such steps provide as we progress.

Following our callings is difficult, which is why we need a firm foundation. That foundation includes faith. In what seems like an acknowledgement of God's hand in this work of becoming ourselves, LeVoy observes "we turn to God when our foundations are shaking, only to learn that it is God who is shaking them—dreams rarely stir up troubles, but acting on them does."

God does not call us to do small or necessarily easy things, but He also does not call us to do things for which we have not been well equipped. This simplifies the task of finding our calling; we should be looking to grow in ways that use our natural talents. The Bible tells us: "We have different gifts, according to the grace given us. If a man's gift is prophesying, let him use it in proportion to his faith. If it is serving, let him serve; if it is teaching, let him teach, if it is in encouraging, let him encourage; if it is in contributing to the needs of others, let him give generously; if it is leadership, let him govern diligently; if it is showing mercy, let him do it cheerfully" (Romans 12:6-8).

Following a calling is never just about ourselves. LeVoy counsels that "the right motivation is crucial. It has to come from a place of true service from a balanced and holistic personality. Otherwise, you are not so much inspiring people to follow you as seducing them." He goes on to say that "Right actions and devoted enthusiasms" ensure God's blessings. Still, since we're surrendering ourselves to something larger than ourselves, things may not work out as we intend. LeVoy's advice is that we should "expect nothing and be prepared for anything." He further advises that it is important to stay open and "listen for further instructions."

Scripture has provided us with a recipe for spiritual success that parallels this advice about finding our callings: serve God, put our faith in Him, take the risks necessary to continue to grow, faithfully steward the talents that God has given us, and focus on His higher purposes—but we are still left with the difficult task of discernment. How can we be sure of God's will?

To be perfectly honest, I don't think we can always be certain. Life can be awfully messy, and sometimes there are no easy answers. For example, I have a friend who perhaps should declare bankruptcy. Everything he has told me suggests that this may be the best answer for him, his family, his business, and his creditors. But, his equity investors would be wiped out, and he doesn't want that.

He is a faithful, hard-working Christian caught in very difficult circumstances. He seems to believe that if he attracts capital his situation will be resolved. From the limited information he has given me, I believe that capital may not be available, given the complexities of the situation, and even if it is, any such capital may only delay the inevitable. He is a faithful steward working furiously to resolve a very tough situation, but if the crisis in real estate continues much longer, all of his efforts may prove to be a waste of his considerable talents and treasure.

The Bible makes clear that God does not want us to waste our talents and treasure.

My friend prays earnestly about his situation; I pray earnestly about his situation; and the evidence suggests that we are hearing God say two very different things. He seems to hear God saying "you were given these resources to steward, and you need to work through this." What I believe I hear God saying is that he may need to lose his attachment to his business. To be honest, though, I have no idea whether he is right, I am right, or whether we're both wrong. Certainly, he is better positioned to discern God's will for himself than I am, provided he is able to detach himself enough from all of the earthly considerations that naturally attend such momentous decisions. It is no easy task, and, despite his faith, devotion and stewardship, his life has been turned almost upside down.

Unfortunately, as this example suggests, discerning God's will for our lives is difficult. Indeed, it may take an entire lifetime. But certainly we can make progress in the meantime. Richard Nelson Bolles, The author of *What Color Is Your Parachute?*, has written a small book that may help us to get started. In his book, *How To Find Your Mission In Life*,[34] Bolles reminds us that we all have the shared mission of bringing "more gratitude, more kindness, more forgiveness and more love into the world," a task "too big for any one individual."

He describes our individual contribution to this mission as having three parts: "(1) to seek to stand hour by hour in the conscious presence of God, the One from whom (y)our mission is derived, (2) to do what you can, moment by moment, day by day, step by step, to make the world a better place, following the leading and guiding of God's spirit within and around you, and (3) to exercise the Talent which you particularly came on earth to use—your greatest gift, which you most delight to use, in the place(s) or setting(s) which God has caused to appeal to you the most, for the purposes God most needs to have done in the world." Succinctly, God's will, our higher calling, is where our "deep gladness and the world's deep hunger(s) meet."

Imagine the implications this type of thinking could have on the world! For example, it is entirely plausible that we wouldn't have a global financial crisis right now if financial executives approached their roles as a sacred trust. True stewards of capital, with a more enlightened view of the health of the firms that employed them, may not have taken on the excessive risk that led so many firms to failure. Mortgage originators may not have recast interest-only mortgages, initially designed for wealthier, better credit borrowers as a way to maximize the housing tax deduction, as an "affordability" product to the poor, because they would have considered not only the potentially negative implications of higher leverage for those borrowers, but also the much higher risk of loss to the ultimate holders of the mortgage. Similarly, fewer variable-rate mortgages may have been sold, because they would not have wanted to expose their customers, many of whom could not afford an adverse interest rate reset, to the greatly increased risk of losing their homes.

The evidence suggests that many of the people originating such mortgages suspected that the loans had significant risk of loss, but since they were selling them to other entities they did not underwrite them carefully. They ignored their own ability to add value to the transaction—their talent of underwriting—and imperiled the firms who relied on that underwriting when purchasing the securities that contained the loans. Unfortunately, the rating agencies who rated the transactions seem to have been more focused on the related fees than assuring that the articulated underwriting standards were met, sidelining their God-given talents as well.

Obviously, the world would be different a different place if we all valued meeting the world's greatest needs, or even simply exercising our God-given talents, as much as we valued "making a million dollars." In trivializing our contributions to this world down to simply "making money," we deny ourselves more important pursuits or perhaps proper stewardship of the tasks right in front of us.

A simple test for a good decision process (not necessarily a good decision) is a "hindsight" analysis. We can consider trying to explain the consequences of our decisions, assuming that the course of action we chose ultimately failed. We can take this approach as we try to discern God's will. We can ask ourselves how we will feel when we stand before Him at the end of our lives. Will we be constructing convoluted explanations for how our work served His purposes, or will we be able to state, confidently and directly, that we were good stewards of the resources He provided and that we heeded His Word and we obeyed His commands? Of course, He will know the truth when we stand before Him, so our finely-honed skills of cleverly disguising or explaining the truth—skills so well-developed that we sometimes fool even ourselves—will not count for anything. We will have to stand in the ACTUAL TRUTH.

Returning to the present, just as in other troubling times, God is at work in the current financial crisis. There is no doubt many high paid and extremely talented people have been given the opportunity to reflect on, and question the wisdom of, their pursuits. These people may be looking for more spiritually-fulfilling outlets for the talents they possess. They may decide the time has come to serve the world differently.

Consider that a quantitative genius, who spent all of his time structuring obscure investments that ultimately did not perform as expected, may now turn his considerable talent to supply chain optimization, bringing potable drinking water to people who have trouble finding clean water to drink. A salesman, who sold the investments, and possibly out of a job as a result, may apply his salesmanship to raising money for the poor. The executive whose only ambition was to make money and retire early, his fortune greatly reduced by the bankruptcy of his former firm, may consider taking a job teaching in the inner city, so that the second half of his career offers psychic returns that the first half never could. The potential that may be unleashed as a result of many people reflecting deeply on the work of their lives could create an extraordinary force for good—larger than any of us may imagine.

God speaks to us through Scripture, the circumstances of our lives, the counsel of other faithful people, and the promptings of His Holy Spirit. Faithfully reconciling those inputs, with the faith that God may expect great things from us, is how we discern our mission in life: the will of God. The Rabbi Harold Kushner cites another writer in offering a simple prescription for us: "We are put here on earth to love, and when we have done that, we have fulfilled our life's mission."[35] Approaching each day with this mission in mind will help us to divine God's will.

DISCUSSION/STUDY QUESTIONS FOR CHAPTER ELEVEN

1. Hebrews 10:36 contains conditional language and cites the need to persevere in order to receive what God has promised. How do we reconcile this verse with the idea that through grace we are saved?

2. Comparatively speaking, it seems much easier to embrace the promises of the loving God of the Bible than the admonishments about Satan and evil. Why is that? What evidence do you see in the world for the existence of evil? Can faith cause us to underestimate its power?

3. How can we be certain that we are doing God's will, rather than using our religion or faith as justification for our own desires? Is there an intersection among the world's great religious doctrines that suggests that God can be found in all of them? How do we bridge the gap between this intersection and the things that divide us?

4. What would God have you do that would not be easy for you? Would you be willing to do it in an attempt to get closer to God? What if you did, but nothing seemed different?

CHAPTER TWELVE

PRACTICE FAITH (FAITH WORKS)

FAITH, BY ITSELF, IF IS NOT ACCOMPANIED BY ACTION, IS DEAD.
(JAMES 2:17)

We have briefly considered the debate down through the ages about faith versus works. The finer points of the debate seem to revolve around collateral concerns about our merit before God and God's infinite mercy, but it seems that we are complicating the matter unnecessarily.

Faith works. Whether to express gratitude for God's grace received, or to attempt to maintain God's good graces, or evidence our receipt of His grace, faith works. For the record, I am in the "expressing gratitude" camp, not the others. We are in God's good graces because of our faith in Jesus Christ, and because of this we have nothing to prove or evidence.

The Bible tells us that "Faith is being sure of what we hope for and certain of what we do not see" (Hebrews 11:1). In the book of Hebrews, we find an incredible summary of people of faith throughout the ages, beginning with Abel, to Abraham, who "obeyed and went, even though he did not know where he was going" (Hebrews 11:8). It continues down the centuries to Moses, who "when he had grown up, refused to be known as the son of Pharaoh's daughter. He chose to be mistreated along with the people of God" (Hebrews 11:24-25). Moses made the difficult choice, although he was unsure about his fitness for the task God had for him. Indeed, Moses was so unsure that he asked God four times to pick someone else for the job, angering God in the process.[36] Ultimately, Moses exhibited great faith and aligned himself with his God-given calling, despite obvious hardship and the seemingly low odds of success.

This concise and exhilarating history has a lot to teach us about faith. The nature of faith is obedience, which requires action—a willingness to go even though we're not entirely sure about where God is taking us, and even though the journey may be hard.

The writer of Hebrews urges us to consider a view much larger than ourselves. He observes that all of the people he mentioned, and many that he did not, "were all commended for their faith, yet none of them received what had been promised. God had planned something better...so that only together with us would they be made perfect" (Hebrews 11:39).

In other words, all of the faithful are part of this incredible plan that has been over four centuries in the making. The key is to think big and to have the courage to become part of that plan. In so doing, we should not imagine small possibilities, because "with God all things are possible" (Matthew 19:26).

In the Bible we're told that we "need to persevere, so that when (we) have done the will of God, (we) will receive what he has promised" (Hebrews 10:36). So, take a step and be determined. You may surprise yourself with what you can do when you cast fear aside and follow God's calling for you.

DISCUSSION/STUDY QUESTIONS FOR CHAPTER TWELVE

1. This chapter, which references one of the great debates among Christians, is deliberately short. What is the point of faith if nothing else changes in our lives?

2. What are three tangible things that you can do to express gratitude for God's blessings?

3. Reflecting on the chapter about surrender, how might doing these things lead to a virtuous circle of deepening faith and consequent actions that results in a closer connection to God?

4. What would you be willing to do to help another person if you were absolutely certain that you would succeed? What reservations do you have about your chances of success? Are there things that you can do to dispel your concerns?

CHAPTER THIRTEEN

SHARING OUR FAITH

"WHOEVER ACKNOWLEDGES ME BEFORE MEN, I WILL ALSO ACKNOWLEDGE HIM BEFORE MY FATHER IN HEAVEN."
(MATTHEW 10:32)

Sharing our faith is an excellent way to grow in our faith. Like anything else, we learn from teaching as much as practicing, and sometimes more, because in teaching we quickly see where our own understanding may be vague. Importantly, we should not wait until we think we have "perfected" our knowledge before being willing to share, because we will be waiting a lifetime. We need to shed the fear of exposing ourselves and our own weaknesses, and become adequate witnesses for our faith. Unfortunately, once we do that, we will be ostracized by some and ridiculed and condemned by others.

We all know a card-carrying, crucifix wearing, salvation proclaiming Christian who is willing to lie, gossip and manipulate to get whatever he or she wants. But we also know that this does not imply that all Christians are hypocrites who ought to be avoided.

Christians are people, and all people, Christian included, are less than perfect. Christians—in particular faithful Christians—try to be wary of falling into the trap of acting differently than we believe, even if we do not always succeed in the endeavor. We recognize that we cannot take God's grace for granted. As Paul exhorts, just because Jesus Christ takes away our sins does not mean that we should go on sinning. Rather, grace instructs us to live in a way that exhibits the grace we have received, facilitating our ability to share our faith credibly. Unfortunately, in choosing to do so, we may still be met by cynicism and stereotyping, because those, too, are attributes of people.

It is November 2008 and the United States has just been through a historic, if at times grueling, presidential election. Reflecting a fundamental optimism that has imbued America since inception, America voted for hope over experience in this election. If that faith is accompanied by sincere effort and a higher vision for America than political retribution and simple income redistribution at the hands of a growing government, then perhaps we can be confident that our nation will continue to live under God's blessings.

My reason for noting these historic times is to provide context for the time of my writing and the message of this chapter. Anyone following the most recent presidential race knows that a lot of focus was placed during this and the last election on the "religious right" and on "evangelicals." Unfortunately, the stereotyping that accompanied this focus has been an abomination. Every Christian, indeed every person, should be concerned about the innuendo and what amounted to outright attacks on people for their faith.

For example, one political commentator, in analyzing Vice Presidential nominee Sarah Palin's likely stance on the environment, said something to the effect of: "well, since she is an evangelical Christian, all else equal, she would not be concerned about the environment, because she hopes for the end of times." Such a statement is utterly ridiculous. The fact that it got reported in mainstream news media without any reflection on the foundations of true Christian belief in this area is appalling and symptomatic of a media that has become an unwitting accomplice in the denigration of people of the Christian faith.

Essentially, Palin was branded by this person as being anti-environment because she is a Christian. In contrast to what was asserted, Christians believe that God gave man a stewardship role with respect to the earth. Indeed, it is one of the first roles God gave us. Nobody in such a stewardship role would be inclined to forsake the planet to hasten the end times. So, in addition to being appalling in its sweeping stereotyping, the logic of the analysis was totally erroneous.

Sarah Palin's candidacy had a number of challenges, not the least of which was that she was pushed onto the national stage without adequate time to prepare for the monumental task ahead of her. But concerns about the implications of her faith for her suitability to the role should not have been among those challenges. Clearly they were, even if not as overtly as in the case of this particular critique. Rather than consider her strong faith and the vocal expression of that faith as evidencing the sort of conviction that may have served the nation well, her candidacy was tainted for these virtues. As her example shows, proclaiming our faith may have consequences. In a secular world, those consequences may not always be good. But the commandment to share our faith remains.

All Christians, Catholic, Protestant, Lutheran, Baptist, evangelical or otherwise, have been given what is often referred to as "The Great Commission." Jesus said, "Therefore go and make disciples of all the nations; baptizing them in the name of the Father and of the Son and of the Holy Spirit, and teach them to obey everything I have commanded you" (Matthew 28:19). Jesus considered this so important that it is one of the last things He said while still on the earth.

Even without the command to do so, we would be inclined to share our faith, because it is of primary importance to us in our lives. We consider it the ultimate gift from God, one that we wish to share with others. The key is for us to do this in a way that doesn't make it seem as though we are trying to stuff our belief down other peoples' throats, pushing people away from faith in Jesus Christ rather than drawing them nearer to Him. In this respect, our actions will speak much louder than our words. After all, the purpose of the commandment is to call people to Christ, to a new and entirely different life, not to cause people to question the authenticity of adherents to the faith.

The unfortunate reality is that we are all sinners, and God's grace does not stop us from sinning. If it did, there would be no free will. And sin is insidious.

Recognizing the possible psychological underpinnings for having Satan take the form of a serpent in the Garden of Eden, it is possible that the metaphor goes deeper than just primitive fears. Snakes slither silently. They move slowly, cautiously, and deliberately, getting close enough to their prey to make a quick and lethal strike. Sin is like that. A casual flirtation becomes an affair. A marital dispute becomes an ugly divorce. Disagreement turns into distain, hatred, and even war. And, yes, Christians can fall victim to all of these things.

Since we are all prone to sin, we need to be extremely careful in approaching people on the subject of our faith, lest the faithful be branded hypocrites and people are turned away. Yet, there are times when we have to speak, even if what we have to say is not popular, or we will participate in sin. Our faith requires us to take a moral stand.

It is a shame that people wish to stifle and trivialize the debate about important subjects such as certain aspects of stem cell research and the separate issue of whether such research should be federally funded by saying that anyone against their position is "anti-science." Being aware that the advances of science may have moral implications is being mindful of the potential for harm, not being close-minded. *Frankenstein*, written by Mary Shelley when she was a teenager, still resonates with us today as an allegory for how science can go wrong. Just because we *can* do something doesn't mean that we *should*. Also, just because science has the ability to do something doesn't mean it should be federally funded, which coerces the participation of conscientious moral objectors against their will.

Sometimes it is hard for us to do the right thing, even when we know it is the right thing to do. Proclaiming Christ, speaking the truth or taking a moral stand can be difficult for many reasons. We don't want to make others uncomfortable. We know that the issues are complex and we don't want to appear judgmental. We sincerely don't know how best to express ourselves; after all, discerning people want to proceed carefully.

Evidencing our faith with our words takes practice, but it can be approached in baby steps. When someone sneezes, if we usually say *"Gesundheit"* or "Bless you," we can instead say "God bless you." After all, it is God's blessings we seek for that person. When something good happens, instead of saying "that was fortunate" or something along those lines, we can say "thank God." In this way, we can acknowledge God working in our lives. Such small steps—I can tell you from personal experience—can lead toward a more fulsome expression of your faith, which soon enough people will realize is a fundamental aspect of who you are.

We cannot lose sight of the objective of God's command. God wishes us to draw people near Him, so that they can participate in His healing and transforming power. It is God who gives us the power to proclaim the Good News, and the Bible tells us that we can rely on that power even when we fear that our own words will fail us.

The third and fourth chapters of Acts provide an excellent example of God's provision from the early growth of the church. Peter and John have been evangelizing after having healed a crippled beggar. All the people are amazed, but the religious authorities of the day feel threatened. Peter and John are seized by those religious authorities and Peter's response, "filled with the Holy Spirit" (Acts 4:8), is to proclaim the Good News of Jesus Christ. We read that the people were "astonished" that "unschooled, ordinary men" (Acts 4:13) could be so courageous, and they begin praising God for the miracle of the healing of the beggar.

In Acts 4:22, we read that "the man who was miraculously healed was over forty years old." As this passage suggests, God is not done with us just because we are at mid-life. In fact, with many of us, He is just beginning, and the changes that we will experience as a result of experiencing God may be nothing less than transformational. We may indeed be completely reborn and regenerated. No wonder we want to sing His praises!

There may be no better way to do this than to put ourselves in the service of others. Give yourself away. Give more of your time, talent and treasure away, and give it to those who can never repay you. Our actions will speak louder than our words. We can work with other Christians, perhaps under the banner of the church or a faith-based mission, to make the world a better place and, as the song says, "they will know we are Christians by our love."

Believe. Proclaim your faith, most especially by living your life more fully. Take the leap and do something bigger than you thought you could ever do. You will be rewarded instantly with an exciting, exhilarating life, you will develop a stronger and ever-strengthening faith, and the Bible promises that you will be rewarded for eternity in ways that cannot be imagined.

DISCUSSION/STUDY QUESTIONS FOR CHAPTER THIRTEEN

1. Why do certain Christian denominations seem to take "The Great Commission" more seriously than others? What are the risks of becoming more "evangelical?"

2. It is very easy to stereotype a group of people based on the behavior of some of them. How might our willingness to do so become an obstacle to our faith? How can we overcome this obstacle?

3. The early church grew through the actions of selfless people embracing the disenfranchised and ministering to their needs. Can we still use this model to grow the church today, or does the modern world demand a different paradigm? What role do you believe you have to play in this?

4. Can you name three modern-day people whom you believe epitomize Christian values? What attributes do they possess that you think distinguishes them? How can you emulate those attributes to become more effective in bringing Jesus to others? Can you approach them as a potential source of strength? Who can you talk to as you try to grow in your faith?

CHAPTER FOURTEEN

GOD'S PLAN FOR US

BE ON YOUR GUARD; STAND FIRM IN THE FAITH; BE MEN OF COURAGE; BE STRONG. DO EVERYTHING IN LOVE.
(1 CORINTHIANS 16:13-14)

Despite some of the things stated in an earlier chapter, I do believe that God intended for some people to be billionaires. Such people may illustrate for us in very tangible ways the extraordinary possibilities of excellent stewardship.

The first "billionaire" of ancient biblical times may very well have been Job. Although we read about several other important patriarchs before getting to the story of Job, we are told that the story itself is difficult to date, and that it likely refers to someone who lived long before it was written down. The study notes contained in two of my Bibles indicate that he may have lived between 1000 and 2000 B.C. The example of his life may be particularly relevant to us in these tough economic times, today.

Do you remember the story of Job? Although most of us are familiar with his story, the details bear repeating.

The reason I refer to Job as a "billionaire" is because we learn early in the story that Job "was the greatest man among all the people of the East" (Job 1:3). This statement is made right after an enumeration of some of his vast possessions, so it seems reasonable to conclude that he was an extraordinarily wealthy person, perhaps the equivalent of a billionaire today.

The very first thing that we learn about Job, in the very first sentence of his story, is that he is a man of great character, "blameless and upright" who "feared God" (which is to say revered God) and who "shunned evil" (Job 1:1). Thankfully, these are qualities that even typical people, not just the wealthy, can emulate.

As the story progresses, we learn that the angels have been presenting themselves before the Lord, seemingly at God's request, and that Satan has joined them in doing so. After discussing Satan's whereabouts—"roaming through the earth and going back and forth in it" (Job 1:7)—God asks Satan whether he has "considered" Job, reiterating the strength of character of the man. Satan's response is that Job is faithful to God because of all that God has given him.

Interestingly, this bit of Scripture teaches us is that Satan himself recognizes God as the ultimate source of our blessings. Who among us hasn't lost sight of that from time to time? But this particular book has a lot more to teach us about the nature of God and the nature of faith than this little tidbit.

Satan tells God that Job would surely curse him "to (his) face" if God were to withdraw His blessings from him (Job 1:11). God's response is to give Satan control over Job's fortunes, provided that he cannot harm Job himself. This Scripture tells us something about God. In the interest of our free will, He gave permission for evil to have its way in the world, but He established limits, maintaining ultimate control of the situation.

Satan is quick to take everything from Job, absolutely everything, including his sons and daughters. Job's response is to mourn, but also to worship and praise God, noting that he came to the world with nothing and that he will, apparently, leave it that way as well. Reflecting his admirable character, we learn at the end of the first chapter of the story that "In all of this, Job did not sin by charging God with wrongdoing" (Job 1:22). Job is right in this, as the devil is the source of his affliction, not God. In a sermon on this passage, our pastor noted that perhaps one lesson of this story is how quickly and completely our lives would become miserable if God were to withdraw the hand of His protection from us.

But Satan is not satisfied, because he has not completely broken Job. In the next instance of the heavenly council, he challenges God again. Satan asserts that Job has not cursed God because God has spared him from harm. In response, "The Lord said to Satan, 'Very well, then, he is in your hands; but you must spare his life" (Job 2:6). Once again, Satan gets to test Job, but God still retains ultimate control.

Satan afflicts Job with boils from head to toe, so severe that Job is literally scraping off his own skin. Job's wife encourages him to "Curse God and die,"[37] to which Job replies, "Shall we accept good from God and not trouble?" (Job 2:10). Although he curses the day that he was born, still Job does not curse God for his condition.

Some of Job's friends come along. Initially, they console him, but in time they are convinced that Job has done something wrong. In what one of my study Bibles refers to as "faulty logic,"[38] they conclude that since sin may cause suffering, then all suffering must be caused by sin. As the study note further elaborates, this is not the message of the Bible. Bad things can and do happen to good people. The purpose of such circumstances may be to evidence faith.

In chapter nine of the book of John, Jesus and his disciples encounter a blind man, and the disciples—using the same logic as Job's friends—ask Jesus "who sinned, this man or his parents, that he was born blind?" (John 9:2). Jesus' response is that "neither this man nor his parents sinned, but this happened so that the work of God might be displayed in his life" (John 9:3). In that case, Jesus healed the blind man, bringing glory to God. In our case, how we react to suffering and difficult circumstances may do the same.

In Job's case, the circumstances of his life, as bad as they were, get worse. Job complains about his life and about the hardness of life in general. He complains about his friends, ostensibly there to comfort him, but who ultimately accuse. He despises his life, considers his life meaningless, and longs for death—but he never gives in to the relentless badgering of his friends. To do so would deny his integrity. In chapter after relentless chapter, Job proclaims his innocence, while his friends assume that he must be guilty of something, even if he has forgotten what it is.

Despite the depths of his depression, Job continues to speak to these men, and he still maintains faith in God, although eventually he wrongly concludes that it is God who has stricken him. Still, believing that, he proclaims, "I know that my Redeemer lives, and that in the end he will stand upon the earth...And after my skin has been destroyed...I will see God" (Job 19:25-26). Although he does not perfectly understand his circumstances, Job does seem to recognize that his suffering is for some larger, unknowable purpose. He tells his friends that "I will maintain my righteousness and never let go of it" (Job 27:6), and "I will teach you about the power of God" (Job 27:11).

Near the end of the book, God chooses to answer Job and his friends. His answer is basically this: "I am God and you are not. I am the mighty Creator and you are not. Do you wish to correct Me?" Job acknowledges that he is unworthy and indicates that he will hold his tongue, but he does not repent of his wrongdoing, so God rebukes him once more. In response, Job expresses his remorse for his accusations against God. He repents, saying that he spoke of things that he "did not understand" and that were "too wonderful" for him to know (Job 42:3).

Imagine that! A person who has lost everything, even his children, recognizes that there is some "wonder" in what has happened to him that is beyond his understanding—not just something incomprehensible, but something "wonderful." Whether the original language has the connotations that our language has or not, the Scripture provides a model for the type of faith that can get us through even the toughest times. However bad our circumstances may be, God may have some good purpose to be achieved through them or perhaps through our response to them.

We never really learn why God permitted Satan to afflict Job, a righteous man, so harshly. Ultimately, God vindicates Job, telling his friends that He is angry with them for their erroneous counsel. He vindicates Job only after Job stops demanding his own vindication. God promises not to deal badly with Job's friends, but only after Job has prayed for them. Job does this, and the Lord makes Job prosperous again, giving him "twice what he had before" (Job 42:10). "The Lord blessed the latter part of Job's life more than the first" (Job 42:12).

Although this book may be useful for some younger people, the title indicates it is especially written for those of us in the second half of our lives. As the story of Job indicates, God's intention is to continue to bless us throughout our lives, as long as we remain open to His blessings. Where we are or how we got here doesn't much matter; what we do now is what matters.

When I started this book, I did it with the intention of writing it and moving on with my life. Since this particular calling also seemed to require leaving behind a lucrative career, it felt burdensome to me. Now, I cherish the work that I believe that God gave me to do. I see it as a significant part of the larger spiritual journey of my life, not something to be done, but a model for how my life can be lived.

Like Job, we can keep our focus on God, even though our circumstances may not be exactly as we would like, and even though we may never entirely understand why our circumstances have brought us to this place. Like Job, we can hold ourselves blameless for the past, not because we are blameless, but because God has declared us blameless, since Jesus Christ has already paid the price for our sins. Like Job, we can trust in God and ultimately be vindicated for our faith.

As they say in Alcoholics Anonymous,™ "Regret for the past is a waste of spirit." God did not equip us with the gift of the Holy Spirit, only to have us waste the opportunities before us. Whether we are eight years old or eighty years old, the rest of our life is in front of us; we are free to live it abundantly, because, like Job, we are washed clean after true repentance. Like Job, we can submit willingly to God and pray that His will be done. And, as in the case of Job, once we have submitted ourselves to God's will, God's blessings really begin to flow.

What does God want from us? The Bible tells us that God wants us to love Him in return. He also wants us to love one another. God wants us to trust Him and to exercise our talents for the purpose of making the world a better place. He wants us to come to faith and to demonstrate that faith in service to others.

For some of us, this may imply radical choices that greatly transform our lives and the lives of others. For others, it may lead to a life of quiet introspection, causing others to think. God made us all different; He gave us all different inclinations and aptitudes. But, at some point, no matter what our natural inclinations may be, we have to encounter the world and offer our talents. We can practice our faithfulness by stretching ourselves a little, every day, and by trying to make the most of what God has given us to steward, no matter how much or how little we possess.

We can start the process by asking ourselves "What do I have to share?" In answering the question, we need to remember the story of the poor widow who put in two coins, worth a fraction of a penny. In nominal terms, the widow put in next to nothing, yet Jesus held her up to all of us as an example of GREAT FAITH. We may think that we do not have much to share, but we all have something. In most cases, we have a lot more to offer than the poor widow. Perhaps, unlike her, we are holding back. I know that I do.

We may worry about the economy or the security of our jobs, so we may give less than a tithe. We may worry about making fools of ourselves, so we may not take chances. We may focus on worldly success, perhaps measuring ourselves by its standards, and in doing so diminish our intrinsic worth as children of God. Recognizing this intrinsic worth increases our sensitivity to others and can strengthen our resolve to express our faith in action.

What does God think of us and what does He expect from us? The Bible tells us that in reflecting on His creation, God thought that it was good, but after the making of the first man and woman, and reflecting again, He thought that His creation was "very good" (Genesis 1:31). What does this tell us? Let's pause for a moment to truly consider the implications of this short bit of Scripture.

Think about the grandeur of a clear, starry night. Spectacular though the heavens are, the heavens are not God's greatest creation.

Consider the beauty of the rising and setting sun. Sunrises can be uplifting, and sunsets can be sublime, but the rising and setting sun is not God's greatest creation.

127

Reflect on the beauty of mountains, forests, deserts and seashores, all of which reveal God's mighty hand. Fantastic though they may be, nature is not God's greatest creation.

Although it is both humbling and ennobling to consider it, man, at his fullest potential, is God's greatest creation. It is man who was created in God's image, not any of these other things. And our precious identity as children of God is reclaimed when our sins are forgiven through faith in Jesus Christ.

God has great plans for us—bigger than anything that we can imagine; and, by the grace of God, we can become part of His plans. However, entering into God's grace—the grace that empowers us to do this—takes faith.

God's plans for us may not align very well with our own plans, or the plans that the people we love may have for us. They may have nothing to do with how much money we earn, how much fame we enjoy or how much prestige is attached to our vocations. And, considering His eternal perspective, God's plans very likely will not provide us with the instant gratification we so often seek.

As earnest seekers, we no doubt have spent a lot of time trying to figure out God's grander purpose for our lives. The story of Job tells us that perhaps we should stop figuring. The answer may be easier than we think. Instead of getting caught up in all of the whys and wherefores of our lives, instead of regretting the past or fretting over the future, we can submit to God's sovereignty and live more fully in the present.

Every single day, in every single situation, we all have a single choice to make. We can be self-centered, putting ourselves and material things first, or we can be God-centered and try to do His will. The first choice is often accompanied by fretting and consternation and, sometimes, by regret. The second choice leads naturally to peace, contentment, and freedom. It empowers us to more faithfully steward our resources and to share our blessings more fully.

All that we need to do is ask ourselves, "What would God have me do in this situation?" After sincerely answering that question, not by conforming God's will to our own, but by sincerely seeking God's will, we can use another question to test the measure of our faith, our response to God, by asking ourselves: "What am I willing to do for God?" Once we have sincerely and faithfully answered that question, then all that we need to do is to do it.

Thank you for taking the time to read this book. God bless you on your journey of faith.

DISCUSSION/STUDY QUESTIONS FOR CHAPTER FOURTEEN

1. In the book of Job, each time we hear about Satan's whereabouts, he is roaming about the earth. If God ultimately controls everything, how concerned should we be with the presence of Satan on earth?

2. Are Job's children the victim of a cruel contest of wills? Why does God permit Satan to persecute Job?

3. Job's friends seem to move from consoling to convicting. What do you think caused this shift?

4. Why doesn't God explain Himself to Job? Why doesn't he explain Himself to us? Is it irreverent to expect such an explanation?

5. Job's vindication comes when he stops demanding it. In what ways are we demanding of God? What can we do to put our demands aside and serve God?

6. What power does our identity as God's children give us to change our lives and our world? How do we access and exercise that power?

ACKNOWLEDGEMENTS

The motto of my college preparatory school is "*Ad Majorem Dei Gloriam*" (AMDG), which means "To the greater glory of God." It seems impossible to write a book about faith without first acknowledging God. To that end, I praise God for the inspiration, the strength and the will to write this book. I have been exceedingly blessed, and I hope to be a blessing to others.

I also want to acknowledge certain others—first and foremost my immediate family, beginning with my wife, Sandy. Sandy, without your love and support, I never could have done this. I recognize how lucky I am to have someone who believes in me and who supports me, no matter what I propose to do. I suspect that most people would be unable to leave the security and the lifestyle that my former employment provided without having their spouses leave them! Instead, you supported my decision, encouraged me throughout the process, and kept after me when my own faith was flagging. I love you, and I thank you.

I also want to thank my children. I can only imagine what an adjustment it must have been to have me constantly around the house after experiencing the alternative. I suspect that it wasn't always easy, especially for my daughter Courtney.

Courtney, watching you grow into the fantastic young lady that you are has been truly amazing. Your courageous and selfless service to your eighth grade Darfur project was one of the milestones in your life that caused me to reflect harder on my own. Your good example provided much of the inspiration that caused me to want to express my faith more creatively.

To my son Riley, your energy, enthusiasm and contagious love are daily reminders of the blessings with which we enter the world and the many other wonders of childhood. You are a remarkable young person, and I have learned a lot from you. I hope one day to become the man that you believe I am.

I have been blessed with exceptional parents. I especially want to thank my mother for starting my journey toward faith. Naturally selfless and service-oriented, you have made the world a better place for many people. Dad, I have always admired your intelligence and talent, and your reaction to the early draft of this work was a blessing. I consider myself very lucky to have the two of you as parents.

I have encountered many people throughout my life, too numerous to mention, who have shaped my thinking and my faith. I am most grateful to you, especially those of you who offered so much support when I told you about my plans. Your enthusiasm was extraordinary, much needed at the time, and very much appreciated.

I have read many excellent books that have helped me to learn things and to overcome obstacles of every kind, including obstacles to faith. Now having written a book, I more fully appreciate that every book is a labor of love. I am grateful to the authors and publishers of the books that I have read and, most especially, to the authors and publishers whose works are mentioned in this book. I am also grateful to Barb Lilland, who edited this book. I appreciate your experience, responsiveness, thoughtfulness, and tact. Of course, I am responsible for any remaining errors or grammatical annoyances.

As suggested above, I have learned that writing a book is quite an undertaking. Writing about a subject as intensely personal as one's faith is perhaps even harder. I have met and talked to several people while writing this book, and I am grateful to each of them. I especially want to thank Tina and Mike Stone, who provided me with very specific and actionable feedback, as well as tremendous encouragement, precisely when I needed it most. There is no doubt in my mind that God is working through the two of you. You may not agree with everything that is in this book, but it is better because of the feedback that you gave me.

I am also grateful to Reverend Dan Meyer for his inspiration, advice and encouragement. His idea to include discussion and study questions was particularly helpful to the finished product. Thank you, Dan, you helped more than you can imagine.

Finally, I want to thank you, the readers of this book. I have always thought that every book I have ever purchased offered me something useful and was well worth the price. I hope that there is a nugget somewhere in here that offers you something to hold onto and that your faith will grow as a result. I would love to hear your reactions. Please feel free to contact me through my web site at www.brionscottjohnson.com to share your experience and insights.

AMDG

BIBLIOGRAPHY

Alcorn, Randy. *THE TREASURE PRINCIPLE: Unlocking the Secrets of Joyful Giving.* Colorado Springs, CO: Multnomah Publishers, 2001.

Bentz, Joseph. *When God Takes Too Long: Learning to Thrive During Life's Delays.* Kansas City, MO: Beacon Hill Press of Kansas City, 2005.

Blackaby, Henry T., and King, Claude V. *Experiencing God.* Nashville, TN: Broadman & Holman Publishing, 1994.

Bolles, Richard Nelson. *How to Find Your Mission in Life.* Berkeley, CA: Ten Speed Press, 1991.

Kushner, Harold S. *Living a Life that Matters: Resolving the Conflict Between Conscience and Success.* New York, NY: Random House, 2001.

LeVoy, Greg. *CALLINGS: Finding and Following an Authentic Life.* New York, NY: Three Rivers Press, a division of Crown Publishers, Inc., 1997.

Pennington, M. Basil. *CENTERING PRAYER: Renewing an Ancient Christian Prayer Form.* New York: Bantam Doubleday Dell Publishing Group, Inc., 1982.

Perry, Tim. *Mary for Evangelicals.* Downers Grove, IL: InterVarsity Press, 2006.

Peterson, Eugene H. *THE MESSAGE: The Bible in Contemporary Language.* Colorado Springs, Colorado: NavPress Publishing Group, 2002.

The Quest Study Bible, NIV®. Grand Rapids, MI: The Zondervan Corporation, 1994.

Smith, Martin L. *The Word Is Very Near You.* Eighth printing. Boston, MA: Cowley Publications, 1989.

[1] The reason for the quotation marks around the word "coincidence" is that it probably was purely coincidence that this sermon followed the conversation with my colleague, but it was no coincidence that I made the association between the two. When we're on the lookout for God, we become much more adept at seeing the many ways that He may choose to relate to us.

2 For Moses' response to God's call, see Exodus 3:11, 3:13, 4:1 and 4:13.

3 Recently, noted author and atheist turned Christian Lee Strobel spoke at our church. In his talk to our congregation, he mentioned that one study of famous atheists showed a pattern of poor relationships and/or a sense of abandonment by their earthly fathers. Apparently, the conclusion of the study was that, given their experience on earth, it was difficult for them to trust in a loving, heavenly father. This helped me realize that genuine empathy for the conditions that might give rise to atheism might be the best way to relate to atheists.

4 I am not the first person to suggest the logical argument presented in this paragraph, but I cannot cite a specific reference for the example given.

5 There are a number of excellent books that explore the historical evidence for Christ's life, death and resurrection. Examples include More than a Carpenter by Josh McDowell and The Case for Christ by Lee Strobel, both of which I have enjoyed.

6 For example, James 2:17 says that faith without works is "dead."

7 See, for example, Psalm 63:1, Psalm 119:174 and Isaiah 26:9.

8 Scripture taken from THE MESSAGE Copyright © 1993, 1994, 1995, 1996, 2000, 2001, 2002. Used by permission of the NavPress Publishing Group.

9 Thanks to Senior Pastor Dan Meyer. Note that this may not be a direct quote.

10 Pennington, M. Basil, CENTERING PRAYER: Renewing an Ancient Christian Prayer Form, New York: Bantam Doubleday Dell Publishing Group, Inc., 1982.

11 Smith, Martin L. The Word Is Very Near You. Eighth printing. Boston, MA: Cowley Publications, 1989.

12 Bentz, Joseph. When God Takes Too Long: Learning to Thrive During Life's Delays. Kansas City, MO: Beacon Hill Press of Kansas City, 2005.

13 Alcorn, Randy. THE TREASURE PRINCIPLE: Unlocking The Secrets Of Joyful Giving. Colorado Springs, CO: Multnomah Publishers, 2001.

14 See Matthew 19:16-23.

15 See Chapter three of Alcorn's book. Example scripture passages supporting this statement include: In Matthew 16:27 we are told that God "will reward each person according to what he has done." In Matthew 19:21, Jesus tells the rich young man "go, sell your possessions and give to the poor, and you will have treasure in heaven." In Luke 14:14, Jesus tells us that if we take care of the poor, the crippled and the lame, we will be "repaid at the resurrection."

16 See Romans 12:5-8.

17 See Mark 12:42ff.

18 Many have argued, and I agree, that monetary policy was recklessly loose, to the point of being "bubble-inducing." The conduct of monetary policy, with its gross manipulation of interest rates, did not even resemble capitalism. Bad regulatory policy with regard to the government-sponsored agencies in the mortgage market is another root cause of the problem. Neither the economic model for these entities nor

---

the distortion in their missions from profitably serving their customers to achieving a rate of home ownership that was inconsistent with the natural state of the economy was consistent with capitalism. Poor regulatory accounting practices are also to blame. Mark-to-market accounting, while theoretically defensible, is impractical during a period of time when markets are not functioning well. It created a self-fulfilling, momentum-gathering cycle of forced liquidations, causing technical "insolvency" based on artificially low prices to lead to actual insolvency, forced selling, still lower prices and more insolvencies. The transparency about valuations that capitalism does require could just as easily been left in the footnotes of the financial statements.

Also featured in the current crisis was the reckless pursuit of profits, without regard to risk, by many financial services firms. The related "profits" and "growth" proved to be illusory. This is not an inherent feature of capitalism, but instead a reflection of poor stewardship at many levels of corporate America, most especially Boards of Directors, and a lack of stewardship on both the lending and borrowing sides of mortgage contracts, perhaps reflecting pride, materialism and greed.

19 www.charitynavigator.org

20 See, for example, Luke 24:15-31, which tells of Jesus visiting two of his followers on the road to Emmaus, after his resurrection. They do not recognize him despite what appears to be a fairly long conversation.

21 Obviously, being Christian, I also believe that one's faith is ultimately perfected by belief in Jesus Christ.

22 Perry, Tim. Mary for Evangelicals. Downers Grove, IL: InterVarsity Press, 2006.

23 See, for example, Deuteronomy 4:2.

24 http://www.merriam-webster.com

25 The Message, page 975.

26 This and the following quotation are from The Message translation.

27 2 Corinthians 1.

28 1 John 3:6 says that "No one who lives in him keeps sinning. No one who continues to sin has either seen him or known him."

29 See 2 Peter 2:20-21.

30 The Quest Study Bible, page 1699.

31 Scripture from The Message translation.

32 Blackaby, Henry T. and King, Claude V. Experiencing God. Nashville, TN: Broadman & Holman Publishing, 1994.

33 LeVoy, Greg. Callings: Finding and Following an Authentic Life. New York, NY: Three Rivers Press, a division of Crown Publishers, Inc., 1997.

34 Bolles, Richard Nelson. How to Find Your Mission in Life. Berkeley, CA: Ten Speed Press, 1991.

35 Kushner, Harold S. Living a Life that Matters: Resolving the Conflict Between Conscience and Success. New York, NY: Random House, 2001, page 152.

36 See Exodus Chapters 3 and 4.

37 Yes, Job's wife really suggested that he should curse God and die. See Job 2:9.

38 The Quest Study Bible, page 682.